SUZETTE'S
DADDY ISSUES

SUZETTE'S
DADDY ISSUES

A Memoir of Violence and Hope

SUZETTE SHANLE

Columbus, Ohio

Suzette's Daddy Issues: A Memoir of Violence and Hope

Published by Gatekeeper Press
2167 Stringtown Rd, Suite 109
Columbus, OH 43123-2989
www.GatekeeperPress.com

Developmental Editor: Vivien Cooper
Cover Design: Elizabeth Dobbs

The editorial work for this book is entirely the product of the author. Gatekeeper Press did not participate in and is not responsible for any aspect of this element.

ISBN (paperback): 9781662901447
eISBN: 9781662901454

Library of Congress Control Number: 2020939328

Dedicated to my family . . .

Mom, John, Ricky, Terry, Jon Paul,
Savannah, Sophie, and my dads.
I love you all.
You each have made me who I am today.
I wouldn't be me if not for each of you.

FOREWORD

A s you are about to find out, I've had daddy issues ever since I was a little girl. That made it hard to find safety and stability in my life. The man in the moon was the only man I could ever really count on to make me feel safe and secure (until I met my husband, that is).

Ever since I was seven years old, I've had a special relationship with the man in the moon. My brother John and I would climb up on top of the boxcars of the train that sat overnight at the factory across from our house in Toledo, Ohio. We loved to lie there at night and gaze at the moon.

Climbing up there at night was perfect for two reasons. For one thing, the ladder on the boxcars that led to the roof was too hot during the day but cooled down around nightfall. And secondly, at night, we could be sure that the trains wouldn't start pulling out of the station with us halfway up the ladder. Sometimes the trains that ran behind our house would go whizzing by with so much force, the train we were lying on would start rocking.

It was fun to look up at the man in the moon and wonder what he was doing that night. I filled hours on end gazing at my familiar friend. When I said my prayers, I would look out the window and say goodnight to the man in the moon.

Often, when our family was driving late at night for hours on end during one of our many moves, I would look up at the moon. And I would know that he was following me from my old home to my new one.

I always felt unsettled in our new houses until night set in. That was the time when I could look up and see the glow of the moon and get lost in thought over what he was doing up there. I knew that others were afraid of the dark, but not me. The daylight was when the worst things happened. I welcomed the night because I knew it meant I would get a glimpse of my tried and true friend and know he was there for me.

ONE

WHEN I LOOK back on my life, I realize that there was never a time that our family stayed put for very long. All the moving around seemed like a fun adventure as a young child. Sometimes it seemed like each place got better. The houses got bigger, or I got my own room, or there was simply the excitement of being in a new state and city or town. Being so young, winning sometimes meant something as simple as getting a new puppy or bedspread.

Sometimes things didn't get better and the house wasn't any bigger and I didn't have my own room. Losing might also mean leaving behind a new friend or a house I had become attached to. I had been taught that this was all part of the give and take of life.

Mom always said, "Sometimes you win and sometimes you lose."

So, I understood that sometimes in life, I would be a winner, and sometimes I would be a loser.

Whenever we first moved to a new place, I found myself in a position where I didn't have any friends. Sometimes I didn't make one friend in the entire time we lived in a place. It was so hard to connect. Other kids had been there longer than I had and were used to playing with each other. I was an outsider and I felt very alone.

When I did finally form a friendship with someone, there was no guarantee that it was going to pan out. In one way or another, I often got the message that I wasn't a good enough friend. Maybe I hadn't lived there long enough, and our relationship wasn't as solid as the ones they had with their other friends. Or, maybe I didn't understand their inside jokes or seem quick-witted enough.

Once in a while, I found a true friend—someone patient and kind who took the time to explain things and didn't make fun of me. A true friend enjoyed my sense of humor and whatever else I had to offer and invested their time in me. On the rare occasions that I found a true friend, I wanted to hold on tight and never move out of the neighborhood. As I got older, and everything at home unraveled, my friends meant more and more to me. I found safety in my friendships.

Each move had its own positives. But they all masked the chaos at the core of our family: my mom's up-and-down relationship with my dad. Once my dad came along, moving got all tangled up with safety concerns. Dad brought his own safety issues into our lives, but that's not what I'm talking about. The danger was posed by Fred, the guy who came along *before* Dad.

I became hyper-aware of the danger and was always on pins and needles, waiting for the phone to ring. I knew that my mom was truly afraid. She was always worried that Fred, the guy who had stabbed her, would somehow find out where she was living and come after her—and us. (More on Fred in a minute.)

I learned early in life that moving was something that was done in a purposeful way. It was always done for a reason that was easy to understand and excuse. When we were moving all the time and hiding out, I took comfort in knowing that Dad (Richard) was with us.

Richard was actually my stepdad, but I always called him Dad. When I first got Richard as my dad, it was especially exciting. A dad was something other people had, and I didn't. I wanted one and now I had one—not that my dad was exactly a walk in the park. It wasn't easy dealing with his verbal and physical abuse, his drinking and his scams. But I don't want to get ahead of myself here.

As time went by, I internalized an understanding of the darkness that followed us, and I carried it with me everywhere we went. Now, moving—the very thing that used to be a fun adventure—became a matter of survival. If we didn't keep moving, something bad could happen, something even worse than my mom getting stabbed.

My bio-father (we called him Daddy John) was employed as a garbage man. He seemed to be the least likely person on earth to end up with my mother. Then again, he was a good-looking Elvis Presley type who wore a leather jacket and slicked back his dark hair. And he was very talkative while Mom was a real bookworm and the smartest girl in school. So, they complemented each other really well.

They met during my mother's last year of high school when she was eighteen and he was nineteen. (I would become their third child.) Although my mom was still in high school at the time, she found herself pregnant, resulting in a situation where her mom had to stuff her into her prom dress. Being as it was the 1960s, Mom felt like she couldn't tell her family that she was pregnant. Shortly after graduation, Mom and Daddy John got married and John, Jr. was born.

Before too long, they had a second son and named him Michael. This was in the days before phrases like physically challenged were used. The baby was called a handicapped, "mongoloid" or "water-head" baby. He only lived a little while, not reaching his second birthday. During that time, he had constant seizures, as many as twenty a day.

This situation was heartbreaking for my mom and Daddy John. It wore them down to the point where it created little cracks in their marriage. Daddy John was ashamed of his little mongoloid baby. He couldn't understand why Mom insisted on keeping the baby at home with them. In those days, mongoloid babies were usually sent away to live in a state home.

Neither of my parents could really take the baby anywhere due to his condition. But Mom was determined to love and nurture her son for as long as he was on earth. So, that's what she did, isolating herself at home with her two young children.

As far as Daddy John was concerned, Mom's refusal to send the baby away was just plain nuts. He told her that it was her fault that the baby was "retarded" because her family was full of crazies. He would say, "My family may be crazy, but your side of the family is eccentric *and* crazy!"

When the baby died, Daddy John's side of the family had a wake. They were drinking, partying and celebrating. This was in keeping with their Polish family tradition. (My bio-father's mother was a Polish immigrant.) Meanwhile, my mom was beside herself with grief. This tradition of partying after a death seemed brutal to her.

While Mom was pregnant with me, she reached the end of her rope and left Daddy John. The way Daddy John handled the trauma of losing the baby really did not sit well with Mom. She ended up coming to the conclusion that they were a mismatch. She couldn't understand Daddy John's ways or his culture.

Mom needed money to hold her over until she could get a job. Luckily, she didn't have to look far. Daddy John was the son of an immigrant mother, who taught him to scrimp and save. So, Mom knew about his habit of hiding his money in the freezer.

TWO

DADDY JOHN WAS so angry over Mom leaving him, he denied his paternity of their unborn baby—me!

Soon after leaving Daddy John, Mom dated Fred. Then she met Richard and decided she wanted to date him instead. Richard lived with his mother, Betty, across the street from the bar where Mom worked.

"You've got to meet my son!" Betty told my mother. "You're single . . . he's single."

So, Mom went with Betty the day Richard was released from prison and met the bus that transported inmates. Mom was struck by Richard's broad shoulders, black hair and piercing brown eyes. The fact that Richard was fresh out of prison must have been fine with my mother. Otherwise, she would have turned tail and run.

As the story is told, Richard's early life involved him going from an orphanage into the military and then into prison. It all started when Betty gave up baby Richard to her parents to raise. Richard acted up and was labeled by his grandparents as a bad seed.

One day he was playing at the cemetery with his half-brother, who was around his same age. As the boys were playing, a gravestone got loose. It fell on Richard's half-brother, crushing him to death. Richard's grandparents blamed Richard for his half-brother's death and sent him to live in an orphanage.

Richard's time in the military also came to a bad end when he got drunk one night and stole a captain's jeep. He served some time in prison for that. Then, later, he did some hard time for killing a man.

Richard had apparently been a pool hustler and killed the man over a game of pool gone wrong. He must have been carrying a lot of buried anger over having his half-brother's death blamed on him.

When Richard got out of prison, he started earning his living by running numbers for the mob. When he and my mom first started dating, she was working for a doctor. (Later, during one of her separations from Richard, she would end up dating the doctor.)

One day after Richard and Mom started dating, Mom went to work. John and I followed Richard over to the bar. We each had a shiny half dollar that Richard's stepdad, Red, had given us. We were very excited—but the day soon took a frightening turn.

Richard was trying to collect from a man who owed him money. When the man wouldn't pay, he and Richard started to argue. Richard had a bottle in his hand and broke it. He wanted the man to think he was planning on using it as a weapon.

Then, while the guy's eyes were on the bottle, Richard used a knife he had hidden in his other hand. He slashed the guy across his face in the spot between his eyelids and his eyebrows. Blood filled the man's eyes and face and he couldn't see. While the man's eyes were bloody, Richard reached into the guy's pocket, and took his money.

I was shocked and a little scared, but Richard had a way of making you feel safe. He seemed to be completely in command, so my fear went away. I was with this strong brawler who protected us and treated us like we were his people. I was happy he was mine and not somebody against me.

Then Richard turned around, threw me on his shoulders, grabbed John by the hand, and casually walked out of the bar with us. It made me happy to be on Richard's shoulders, with my little frilly dress billowing around his neck and shoulders. I felt like he was proud of me.

"Did you learn anything?" he said to John.

"Yeah . . . don't trust your friends."

"No. The hand is quicker than the eye!" That was all he said about that.

Then it was over, and we went and had ice cream. I quickly came to think of Richard as Dad, as he put me on his shoulders and carried me around. Mom and Richard were still in the dating stage, but he stepped up and became the first man to show us that he cared enough to spend time with us. This was our dad!

Dad was big and scary but I thought he was cool looking. I had never had a dad before, so having this man spend time with us was huge.

Mom and Dad were now an item and were together most of the time. They would end up marrying a total of three different times, the first time being after a short courtship when I was about two years old.

Fred was still obsessed with Mom and did not take kindly to her being with a new man. One morning when I was two years old, Mom was in the kitchen. My brother John, who was five at the time, was sitting at the kitchen table, eating a bowl of cereal.

Fred came to the back door.

Without any fear, Mom answered the door, saying, "Hello, Fred. What do you want in coming here?"

"I just want to talk to you for a minute," he said.

"Sure. You can come in and talk to me," Mom said, opening the door, "but just for a minute. I'll pour you a cup of coffee."

When Mom turned her back to pick up the coffee pot, Fred took out a knife and stabbed her in the back. Fred was a short racetrack jockey (and he wouldn't be the last racetrack jockey in my mom's life, either). Being small didn't keep him from doing some real damage.

When John saw Fred stab Mom, he started screaming his head off. This got the attention of Dad (Richard), who had spent the night and was still upstairs. He ran downstairs, yelling to John to call the police. Then he pinned Fred to the floor and held him there until the police could arrive. (Given Dad's violent past, he could have easily killed Fred.)

Mom lost a lot of blood as well as her spleen. She needed extensive hospitalization.

I have a vague memory of that day—the chaos, the screaming, the blood. I later learned that Fred asked the police whether Mom was still alive as they were pulling away in the squad car.

"Yes, she's still breathing," said the policeman.

"Well, I wanted her dead!" said Fred.

My mom always insisted that I was Daddy John's daughter—until I turned nineteen or so. Then she planted a seed of doubt in my mind. It was devastating for me to even contemplate the *possibility* that Fred might be my bio-father. He was a horrible man who tried to murder my mother and kept our family on the run for years.

(Later in life, I would wonder, *Is that why Dad treats me so badly? Is it because he thinks I'm Fred's? Does he think I'm a bad seed, the way they thought he was when he was a kid?*

In my heart of hearts, I knew it wasn't true. As far as I was concerned, there was no way on earth that Fred could be my father. I knew that I belonged to Daddy John. For the most part, I put the idea of Fred being my bio-father out of my mind.)

The sad thing was, Daddy John never claimed me as his daughter. It seemed likely that Mom was already pregnant with me before she met Fred. So, I never understood why Daddy John couldn't accept me as his daughter. He proudly welcomed my brother John into his home and family—but never me. It would only be much later in life that he was welcoming and loving toward me. Even then he never said out loud that I was his and he was mine.

Mom had the State of Ohio looking into whether or not she was a fit parent. This investigation was based on the fact that my mom was romantically linked to both Dad and Fred. In those days, the state considered it unacceptable behavior for a single mother to have two men in her life. And both Dad and Fred had criminal records. Fred was charged with attempted murder for stabbing Mom, and Dad had already served time for murder.

While they were investigating the matter, the authorities decided that it was best for us kids if they removed us from Mom's custody. Meanwhile, Daddy John was also trying to take us away from her. It was really John, Jr. that he was after but we were a package deal. When Mom hid one of us, she hid all of us.

In order to stay one step ahead of the authorities and Daddy John, Mom kept us constantly on the move. Every two or three days, she had someone pick us up and move us to a different safe house. This went on until Mom healed sufficiently from her stab wounds.

When Mom finally returned home after spending a month in the hospital, she was both physically and emotionally stronger. "You're not taking my kids!" she told Daddy John.

When I was a little girl, I was so shy and quiet, it hurt to talk. When I did work up my nerve to say something, the words coming out of my mouth sounded all wrong. I never felt like I was speaking properly.

This awkwardness and self-consciousness stemmed from an incident that happened when I was four or five years old. My mother had taken my brother John and me with her to the hospital to visit our grandma.

When we reached the hospital parking area, I said to my brother, "Want to race?"

"Yeah!" he said.

We set off running, and as the race continued, I found myself on a ramp. We kept running, but now I was at a higher elevation than John. I was running and laughing, thrilled that I was beating my brother in a race, for once.

John saw what was coming and stopped dead in his tracks, assuming I would stop too.

Instead, I ran smack into a concrete wall and was knocked out cold.

Mom picked me up, turned around, and carried me right into the emergency room of St. Vincent's Hospital where we had just been visiting Grandma Margaret. They kept me for a week and put me through a bunch of tests. They discovered that I had Traumatic Brain Injury (TBI). These types of injuries are common among football players.

"Her brain is swelling and she has frontal lobe damage," the doctor explained.

This sent cold chills up Mom's spine, who was still traumatized over the death of her brain-damaged son, Michael.

I always felt like I thought and spoke differently than other people. My decision making was always a little bit off and it gave me a learning deficit too. Growing up with TBI wasn't easy. I learned to cope—but knowing that people thought I was stupid made me extremely self-conscious and a little bit paranoid.

A handful of years ago, I had an MRI following a car accident. The doctor told me that he could see the damage I sustained when I ran into that concrete wall as a kid. All these years later, it is still evident.

In 1968, my little brother Ricky was born in Toledo, Ohio. We were living in the Willis Park Projects at the time. The projects were a cluster of eight-unit buildings, very close together. I really liked having all those people so nearby because it meant that I had more playmates.

When Ricky was a baby, he cried all the time. We came to find out that he had inner ear problems and that's what was making him cry. So, Mom would put Ricky in the baby swing, and give me a nickel for every time I cranked it up. I tended to wander off—until I heard the sound of the ticking that happened every time the swing was winding down.

Then I would go racing back into the room and wind it up again. I wasn't about to miss the chance to get another nickel. I was already a mini-entrepreneur and I loved getting my hands on money. My motto was always, *Anything for a buck!* (Well, not anything, but I was never afraid to work for it.)

Giving birth to Ricky messed with Mom's hormones and she had some sort of post-partum situation going on. Dealing with Dad's hot temper was never easy for Mom. It must have been doubly hard while her hormones were so out of whack.

Mom and Dad were fighting a lot. One night, John and I were upstairs. We heard the door slam really hard. Then we heard the door open again, and more yelling. Then there was dead silence—and then a screaming fight.

My brother and I curled up at the top of the stairs, looking down. We quietly worked our way toward the stairway, and snuck down a few steps so we could hear. We were always worried about what Dad might do to our mom. We didn't want our parents to see us so we stayed tucked away, but that meant we couldn't see too well ourselves.

After hearing a bunch more yelling, we peeked around the corner of the stairs, just in time to see blood. Mom had picked up a unicorn statue to throw at Dad. It broke in her hand and hit an artery. Now blood was squirting out of her hand. I just about passed out. Being so little, I wasn't used to seeing someone bleeding like that.

Dad grabbed a towel and wrapped Mom's hand. Then he left John in charge of me and Ricky and rushed Mom to the hospital. That was the last straw between them—for the moment, anyway. They were always breaking up and getting back together.

Not long after that, Mom found out that Dad had cheated on her with a stripper. When Mom confronted Dad, he got so mad, he left her. I don't know what *he* was mad about when he was the one cheating. I guess he was mad over getting caught. But what did he expect? He was a married man with a stripper girlfriend!

After Dad cooled off a bit, he tried to come back but Mom wouldn't let him back inside. Now, he was really furious. He poured gasoline outside the perimeter of our apartment and threatened to kill us all. Mom had to call the police on him.

That night, as the police put Dad in the squad car and began to drive off, he set off a cherry bomb in the squad car, making them think he had shot himself.

Mom and Dad stayed separated for a while. We left the Willis Park Projects and Mom got us a new place to live. She took her earnings from her job at the doctor's office and made a rent-to-own deal for a house on Auburn Street. Ours was the fourth house from the end on a dead-end road. A group of Hell's Angels lived on the corner of Bancroft and Auburn about half a block away.

It was a three-bedroom house with an upstairs, and it had a railroad track running both in front and in back of the house. Mom turned the study into her bedroom. The place was disgusting on the inside. I would think to myself, *What are we doing here in this awful place?*

My mother must have looked at the house the same way she looked at men—she saw their potential instead of their flaws. And she was handy. So, we all got buckets and blankets and got busy. We hung blankets over the windows, scrubbed the place from top to bottom, and painted the walls. Mom was Superwoman, fixing up the house while working full time.

Mom and Dad remained separated while we were living in that little fixer-upper house. Since Mom worked as the secretary to a doctor, she was gone a lot. (Before she worked for the doctor, she had worked as a secretary at the Penn lightbulb factory.) Mom even dated her doctor boss for a little while during her separation from Dad. Sometimes the doctor took her to New York with him for days at a time.

Every day, Mom got dressed and gorgeous before she went off to work. She never went a single day of her life without makeup, and always spoke graciously. She was also intelligent and wise, and people often turned to her for advice.

Mom was a hard worker and loved us kids, but she wasn't terribly affectionate. But at least she never got rid of us. I knew that my aunt Peggy had left all four of her kids with her husband so that she could pursue a career. Knowing that about my mom's sister made it all the more valuable to me knowing that Mom never left us.

I would hang on Mom and chase her down the road any time she tried to leave the house. I never wanted her to go. She may have needed time to herself. After all, she was only in her twenties, divorced from Daddy John, separated from Richard, and probably traumatized from being stabbed by Fred.

After school and when Mom was out of town with the doctor, she would have Grandma Margaret come over and stay with us kids. Having Grandma Margaret over was a dream. Since Mom loved us but never showed much affection, I was craving the touch of a mother figure. I longed to have Grandma reach out and touch my hair or my shoulder.

Grandma was raised in a convent, was very religious, and read the Bible all the time. And, she was sweet, kind, and loving. But I got the impression that she didn't like girls as much as boys. She favored my brothers to a sickening point and spoiled them rotten. Still, the affection she did give me was more than I was getting from Mom, and I ate it up.

Mom told me that when she was born, Grandma was so disappointed that she wasn't a boy, she wouldn't even look at her for days. Grandma was planning on having a boy and had already chosen the name

Lawrence Robert. When my mother turned out to be a girl, Grandma named her Laura Roberta.

My great-aunt Ethel was also around quite a bit when we lived in the house on Auburn Street. It was obvious that she didn't like us children, even though we were her own flesh and blood.

Mom would take us to pick up Aunt Ethel and bring her to our house. The minute my aunt got in the car, she would say, "Be quiet! Children should be seen and not heard." She didn't understand how hard it was for kids to be quiet.

She was a big blonde lady who wore sparkly dresses and boas in the middle of the day. I thought she was movie-star glamorous and very cool. Whenever she came over, she would spend the whole day with us, and Mom would style her hair. While Mom was doing Aunt Ethel's hair, they talked constantly.

My room was right above Mom's room. I would put my head down to the heat register in the floor to try to hear what they were saying downstairs.

That day on the way to our house, Aunt Ethel had told Mom, "Really blonde! I want it *really* blonde this time."

"It can't take to be much blonder," Mom had said. "It's already white!"

Now, with my ear pressed to the register, I could hear Aunt Ethel saying, "It's falling out! Look . . . it's falling out onto the floor!"

Mom must have over-processed my aunt's hair so she could get it super blonde.

I started giggling. I thought to myself, *She got what she deserved for being mean to us kids!*

I went downstairs to investigate and found Aunt Ethel with her hair wrapped in a turban. Her nose was turned up all snooty but she and my mom were gabbing like nothing had happened.

After that, Aunt Ethel wore a turban for a couple of months. Since she didn't need her hair done during that time, she stopped coming over. *Good riddance!* I said to myself.

I guess I liked the stories about Aunt Ethel better than the actual woman.

THREE

T HE HELL'S ANGELS lived on the corner opposite a body shop. We lived in the middle of the block. One day, a son of one of the Black Panthers broke into the body shop owned by a white man named Mr. Price. He lived on the corner.

Mr. Price took a BB gun and shot the boy who had broken into his body shop. Unfortunately, the BB hit the boy in the eye.

The Black Panthers came into our neighborhood to retaliate. Mr. Price was outside with his big hedge clippers, working on his rosebushes at the time. He had an amazing rosebush garden.

A big car had pulled up in front of our house and sat there with the engine idling. They just happened to be in front of our house—but they weren't there for us. Three Black Panthers wearing velvet bell-bottom pants and big hats got out of the car. They were all holding big-barrel machine guns. Thankfully they started running in the opposite direction, toward the corner.

We lived in Hell's Angels' territory and the Panthers were now on their turf. So, when the Hell's Angels saw the Panthers coming, they turned out in force. The streets filled with gunfire and the windows of our house shook.

My brother John and I were outside playing at the time. When Grandma heard the commotion, she ran outside with a broom and started swatting at us, yelling, "Get inside this house right now! Go upstairs and lay down on the floor. And don't get up until I tell you!"

From inside our house, I could hear the sound of machine guns, cars screeching, and motorcycles. My heart was jumpy over all the sounds.

By the time it was all over, the Hell's Angels had run the Black Panthers out of the neighborhood. Some of the Panthers even left their cars behind. The rumble between the Panthers and the Angels got so bad, the police refused to come down.

Right next door to us lived a morbidly obese couple and their kids. The father was heavy but he was able to get around and go to work. He supported the household while the mother lived in her bed. She was never seen downstairs.

I felt so badly knowing that this woman was too heavy to leave her room. I couldn't imagine never being able to go outside, or watch her kids run and play, or help with their homework. She was too heavy to engage in life.

There were three kids in their family—one girl my age, a boy around John's age, and another boy younger than me. When the kids and I were playing together, I would run in and out of their house like they didn't have parents. Their mom would be upstairs because that's where she lived. Their dad would be at work.

At that age, I never understood why the parents' mattress was on the floor or why it was big enough to cover the entire floor. It wasn't until I became an adult that I understood. The morbidly obese mother probably weighed over four hundred pounds. She would have broken a bed.

When I later saw the movie *What's Eating Gilbert Grape?* I thought, *Oh, my gosh! There are other people in the world like that?*

One time I was at their house, sitting at the kitchen table, eating a peanut butter sandwich with the kids. The dad was at work at the time and the mother was upstairs in her bed, as usual. The boy around John's age saw me chewing with my mouth open and punched me in the mouth.

It was shocking to be sitting there one minute, eating a sandwich with my little friends, and to be on their kitchen floor the next, knocked out cold. I left, dazed, and never went back to eat with them again.

The kids may have inherited the tendency for violence from their mother's side of the family. Their mother had a sister who lived a few doors down. The two women hated each other. I was told when we first moved there that our neighbor, the obese woman, had years earlier hit her sister in the head with a hammer.

It made no sense to me that we were allowed over at the home of the violent obese lady and her kids. Yet, we were forbidden to go near the home of the kids' aunt, the victim of the hammer assault. We would have been safer at the victim's house. I guess that's human nature—people trust their neighbors just because they live next door.

Thanks to the bad blood between the kids' mom and their aunt, the children were not allowed to acknowledge their cousins. They couldn't even utter their names. It was the weirdest thing I'd ever seen.

When the Apollo landed on the moon, we were living in the Auburn Street house. We all sat around our black-and-white T.V. set and watched a man walk on the moon. It was proof that the man in the moon was real. I saw it with my own eyes on T.V.

There was always some kind of trouble brewing in the Auburn Street neighborhood. For my brother John and me, trouble met us every day when we walked to school.

The only way to get to our Catholic School was to walk under an overpass. When we emerged on the other side, the Gonzales kids were usually waiting to beat us up and take our milk money. Mom paid our lunch money to the school in advance, so at least they didn't get that. Still, it was no fun getting beat up every day.

Unfortunately, we didn't know any other route to take to get to school. Mom went to work early in the morning, so she was unable to give us a ride.

My brother John would stand in front of me and protect me like a junkyard dog. He was strong and tough, and he would push down the mean kids as they came at us. I appreciated my brother's fighting spirit, but we still got our money taken. After all, there were seven of them and only two of us.

We told our mother that we didn't want to go to Catholic school anymore. It wasn't just the walk to school that we hated, either. It was also the fact that John struggled with the Catholic school rules. He was always in trouble with the nuns.

We figured that, if we went to public school instead, he would get away from the nuns and we would get away from the bullies. Mom worked hard and wanted the best school for us and, as far as she was concerned, that was St. Anne's Catholic School.

John became even more rebellious as he got older and was often in trouble at school. As an act of rebellion, he grew his hair long and refused to cut it. So, his teacher put a ladies' bobby pin in the front of his hair. And one time, I was in class when I saw John through the little window in my classroom door. His teacher had my brother by his ear and was dragging him down the hallway.

It was John's rebellious streak that finally got us out of getting beat up on the way to school. One day, he took some chalk and wrote "Fuck You!" in big letters on the brick wall of the church at school. Not surprisingly, he was expelled.

John's naughty behavior turned out to be a big blessing. Mom had me transferred to the same public school that John was now attending. That was fine with me. We didn't have to face those bullies on the way to school anymore.

In the classroom, I was quiet and did what I was told, but reading was a struggle. I had a lazy eye and always wore glasses. In first grade, I also wore a black patch to correct my lazy eye. I was very self-conscious, thanks to the glasses, the eye patch, me being plain looking, and the learning difficulties that were brought on by my brain injury.

I was not a pretty girl. I had a lazy eye, mousy-brown hair and one front tooth until I was about seven years old. I wouldn't grow into some kind of pretty until my mom made me go to modeling school later in life. Being a tomboy, I had to learn how to be girlie. I preferred bell-bottom jeans and dirt bikes, but Mom knew she needed to get me ready to be a proper girl.

I was embarrassed that I was a poor reader, so I never volunteered to read in class. Thanks to my brain injury, math was also hard for me. Mom would sit with me and a pack of flash cards and try to help me with math problems. It was no use. Even when my mother repeatedly showed me the same card, I had trouble retaining the information.

Mom would get frustrated with me and say, "We just went over that! I don't understand why you can't remember!"

I wasn't great with my schoolwork but I did love social studies and I was very good at art. I developed techniques to get out of things that were hard for me at school. I would say that I needed to be excused to go to the bathroom. Or, I would tell the teacher that she looked pretty that day. Mom called this manipulation but I thought of it as good survival skills.

FOUR

D AD KNEW A man from prison named Jack. During a period when we were in transition, Mom and Dad took us to stay with Jack and his wife, Inez. They had five kids and a two-story house with an upstairs attic they had turned into a playroom. The house was filled with kids of all ages, big and little.

I loved staying there. We would play for so long, we would drop wherever we landed and fall asleep. One of my favorite things about staying with Jack and Inez was the sounds in their house. The wooden floor in the kitchen, for example, made a creaking sound whenever I would pass by the fridge. Being an old Victorian house, it seemed to have a life of its own.

One night, I fell asleep on the couch. I woke up to find Inez's older son with his hands all over me like an octopus. Somehow, while I was sleeping, he had wriggled under me. I pretended to be asleep and faked rolling over in my sleep.

I was scared. I was only seven years old and starting second grade and this boy was a teenager. I never wanted to tell anyone. I didn't want them mad at me, and I didn't want the boy's mom mad at my mom and dad. So, I never talked about what happened.

It was a one-time violation. If it had happened repeatedly, I'm sure I would have felt differently about it. I said to myself, *Who cares to hear it, anyway?*

I knew that what this boy did was wrong. I knew it was a violation. But I let all the good things that happened in Jack and Inez's house override my memories of that violation.

One time, Mom and Inez took all eight of us kids to a restaurant together. "Oh, I see you brought the daycare!" said the hostess, looking at the big group of us.

"This ain't no daycare!" said Inez. "Them black ones is mine, and them other three's hers."

Later in life, Mom and I were driving by Jack and Inez's old house. I finally told her about Inez's boy touching me.

I said, "Sorry I never told you, Mom. I knew it would have affected your friendship with Jack and Inez, and I didn't want to do that."

Mom just quietly took in what I was saying. She didn't comfort me or seem outraged on my behalf. All she said was, "Try to think of something good, Suzette."

I took her mild reaction as shock. I figured she needed some time and would talk to me more about it later. We never did talk about it again.

From Mom's example, I learned to avoid looking at the bad things that happened in the past. I keep what was good and look to the future. Yet, I know that we are all products of our past. Take Grandma Margaret for example. During the war, Grandma's mother had to place all of her kids into different orphanages. Her husband may have been away in military service.

Grandma and her sister Mary were sent to an all-girl convent orphanage. (I met Mary only once. She lived far away in California.) The two girls were mistreated. Mary had sewing-machine oil squirted in her ear because she wasn't sewing fast enough. From then on, she was deaf in one ear. She and Grandma lived in the orphanage until they were old enough to leave and live on their own.

The orphanage burned down and that's how she finally got out of there. Her records were in the orphanage and burned in the fire, so she had to guess at her actual age. Grandma carried the imprint of the orphanage inside of her. She was religious, frugal, proper and quiet. Miraculously, despite being abused, she also turned out sweet, loving and kind.

This tells me two things. Yes, we are products of our past—but we also have free will and can choose to be good people.

We stayed with Jack and Inez for less than a month. When we left, we went to a house that was really close to theirs. Our new home was a two-story Victorian duplex. We lived in the enormous upstairs. (I am not sure who lived downstairs.) The kids who lived next door were mean but at least they were kids. I was happy to have playmates.

Our new house felt really safe, especially because we were away from Jack and Inez's teenage boy. The house had hardwood floors and heat registers that looked like pieces of furniture. If you touched them, you would burn yourself. If my brothers and I were feeling ornery, we'd push each other into them when they were hot.

It was in this house that my mother pierced my ears by placing a potato behind each ear and using a needle and a string. Mom also used to curl my hair with a metal rod that got extremely hot—so hot that steam rolled off of it. I had extremely fine hair that was hard to comb. So, Mom was often pulling my hair without meaning to. Or, accidentally burning me with the curling iron.

My mother didn't have the patience to sit and style my long hair. She was always in a hurry. Any time we were walking together, she would get going so fast, I couldn't keep up. She would pull on my arm until it hurt and say, "Come on! Come on!"

Without the patience to style my long hair, Mom decided to put her brief beauty school training to good use and give me a pixie cut. Since Mom didn't quite know what she was doing in terms of hair cutting, my hair came out pretty choppy—but I loved it. At least that put an end to Mom trying to comb my long, fine, stringy hair, or curl it with a hot iron that always burned my ears.

I loved it when my mother told me stories about Grandma working in beauty salons during the Great Depression. (I heard some of these stories from Grandma too.) Grandma didn't have any experience or licensing to work as a hair stylist, but none was required in those days. These were stories about the beauty salons in the time of the Great

Depression when no one really had the money to pay their beautician. So, people paid Grandma with S&H Green Stamps or government vouchers.

A lot of customers were willing to give up the stamps that were allocated for shoes if it meant a chance to have their hair done. They would barter using whatever they could get their hands on in those days—stamps, livestock, whatever. By styling hair, Grandma was able to feed Mom and Aunt Peggy.

"There wasn't a lot of money to go around," Grandma explained, "but the times were so hard that the ladies would do anything to get their hair done up pretty to make them feel better."

Salons in those days had these perming machines that came down from the ceiling and had big metal clamps with electric current running through them that fit over the customer's perming rods.

One day when Mom slowed down long enough to curl my hair, I said to her, "Someday, I want to do hair like you and Grandma!"

"If you do hair," my mom told me, "you'll always have food and whatever else you need. And who knows? Maybe someday you'll tell your own daughters stories about you doing hair and they will want to carry on the tradition too!"

Later in life, I would find out that Mom and Grandma really knew what they were talking about. I went on to work as a hair stylist for thirty years and was always able to support myself. Until I got arthritis in my hands and had to stop doing hair, my clients remained very loyal to me. In fact, a handful of my ladies were hard to shake. Most of my clients are still my friends to this day.

My career as a hairdresser may have also been sparked by a doll I had as a child. My doll was named Velvet and my cousin Maria had Velvet's sister doll, Crystal. We were given them for Christmas. (Later in my twenties, I found a Velvet doll at a flea market and bought it.)

These dolls were the size of the popular American Girl dolls and had hair growing out of the top of their heads. I pulled on the hair so it would come out and be long enough for me to cut. Now, whenever I catch my girls cutting their dolls' hair, I try to snap a photo of them when they're not looking.

One day at that same house, the neighbor kids came knocking on our door. That was the first time they had ever asked us to come out and play.

"Our dog just had puppies! Want to see?" they said, leading us into their backyard. Then they said, "Why don't you get a few out and we will play with them."

I kneeled down in front of their German Shepard's doghouse. The mama dog was so big, she filled the entire doghouse. When I reached in and grabbed one of the puppies, I woke up the mama dog. Before I knew what was happening, she had her entire jaw around my head. Thankfully, when I dropped the puppy, she let go.

If I had stopped and thought about it when the neighbor kids first knocked, I might have realized that you shouldn't go near puppies when they are so little. And, I might have even realized the kids' mom had probably told them as much. But I was gullible. I paid for it with a scar above one eyebrow and under my chin—a little souvenir from the mama dog.

I watched a lot of T.V. shows like *Father Knows Best, Leave It To Beaver, I Love Lucy* and *The Addams Family*, and that's where I learned some of my morals. Too bad I hadn't remembered Master Po from Kung Fu saying, "Slow down, Grasshopper!" before I stuck my head in the doghouse.

FIVE

JOHN AND I were usually alone after school. It was just the two of us, doing our chores. We fought a lot. I would tease him and he would explode. I learned to push his buttons and enjoyed the reactions I got. One day we were at home alone, arguing, and he punched me in the face. I wore glasses for a lazy eye, and his punch snapped them right in half at the bridge.

"If you tell Mom and Dad, I'm gonna beat the shit out of you!" he warned.

Ricky was in daycare at the time, Mom was at work, and Dad was at the bar, playing pool. Dad sometimes called Mom at work twenty times a day, bugging her. He would obsess over her and stalk her by phone. He used the excuse that he missed and loved her.

Then, when Mom got off work, she went down to the bar. Once she got to the bar, she spent a lot of her time trying to get Dad to come home before he started fights. Dad was usually busy hustling pool and running numbers.

I knew that John wasn't kidding about beating me up. Even before we moved to this house, he had been pushing me down on the floor and pounding on my chest. By now, he had ramped things up to the next level. I didn't want to get beat up any worse. So, I never mentioned anything to my parents about the fact that John punched me in the face and broke my glasses.

For weeks afterwards, whenever Mom and Dad asked me where my glasses were, I played dumb. I said that I must have left them at school.

Then one day around that time, Dad wanted to play the radio. It wouldn't turn on. He assumed that the batteries needed replacing, so he removed the back. There they were inside—my broken glasses. John must have hidden them in there. I had no idea my glasses were in there. I assumed my brother had thrown them in the trash.

When Dad found my glasses, he assumed that I had known they were in there all along. So, he beat me for lying. I could have ratted out John, but then I would have gotten three beatings over the same incident—the one I already got from John when he punched me in the face, the one I got from my dad, and an extra beating from John for ratting him out.

John was ornery but he was so good looking that girls would follow him around like he was the Pied Piper. I have always loved him and was close to him. He is my brother and that's all there is to it. But I had to be guarded around him.

He was a sweet guy if he knew you and cared about you. He loved all his girlfriends and bought them sweaters and flowers. But he wouldn't think twice about beating a person up, and that included me. Once he even peed on a kid after beating him up.

I noticed John getting super tough after camp one summer. Some boys cut up his black Gentle Ben bear—a medium-sized plush bear he'd had for a long time. He was devastated when he walked in the door with that shredded bear.

Mom did her best to sew it back together and managed to get one ear put back on. But John was devastated. It was after that that he began acting out and becoming a bully.

One day, Mom came to pick me up from school. Instead of driving me home, she pulled up in front of a house I didn't recognize.

"Where are we going?" I asked.

"Shirley's house," Mom said. "Richard and I had a fight . . ."

Mom took us kids and moved us into Shirley's huge two-story house. This was the first time I had ever met Shirley, my mom's friend who would become my godmother and Ricky's. (We were both baptized at the same time.) The entire time we were at Shirley's house, Mom and Dad were apart. This was during one of their separations.

Shirley had six kids. Even with all those kids, she still had plenty of room for Mom and us kids. She was divorced from her husband, Henry, and they had a cordial relationship. I thought it was odd that they were divorced but didn't fight. I also found it strange that he was willing to play hide-and-seek with us kids. I didn't realize that dads even *could* play hide and seek.

I thought Shirley was absolutely beautiful, with a complexion like Cher and a straight, shoulder-length haircut like Marlo Thomas in *That Girl*. There was never a dull moment at Shirley's rambling house, with kids running around. It was great playing with her daughter, Bonnie, who was around my own age.

Shirley sunbathed naked in the backyard, with a little clothesline curtain made of picnic table sheets strung around her for privacy.

Whenever I saw her, I'd laugh and say to Bonnie, "Oh, my gosh! There goes your mom again!"

Then we would run upstairs and find a window so we could peer down at Shirley. We thought it was so funny to see someone her age sunbathing naked.

My mom was so conservative, she wouldn't have been caught dead in a lowcut dress. Yet, Shirley thought nothing of lying naked in the backyard.

Shirley was sweet but very strict. When a Beatles album went missing from the house, Shirley called us kids to attention. She had us line up in a row like little soldiers—her five younger kids and me, John and Ricky.

"Everyone's getting a spanking," Shirley said, "until one of you confesses and admits you took the album."

We all shot looks at each other, waiting for the culprit to save the rest of us from an undeserved spanking. When everyone remained mute, Shirley put us over her lap, one at a time, and gave us two swats with a belt. She was not a small woman and her swats stung and left a red mark. It was terrifying to know that someone other than my parents was going to beat me, but I'd taken worse beatings.

Whoever had taken the album was perfectly willing to watch the rest of us suffer for this crime we didn't commit. I figured her teenage daughters must have taken the album somewhere.

Shirley's oldest boy, Clifford, was in his twenties and rarely came out of his room. He was introverted and loved to sketch. Later in life, he became an art major. I had never seen anyone draw before then and had never known anyone who drew. It was fascinating to see him drawing landscapes and nudes whenever I was lucky enough to catch a glimpse of him.

I had always loved art when I was young and I was much better at it than math, English, reading or writing. I loved to color.

Any time Mom saw me coloring, she would encourage me to stick with it. She said, "You could be an artist if you work on your skills."

Knowing there was at least this one area where I excelled and had talent made me feel good and helped build my confidence. Later in life, I would go on to get a bachelor's degree in art.

Shirley's son, Henry, Jr., was the same age as my brother John, and they liked to run around town together, wreaking havoc. I felt like Henry, Jr. was a bad influence on John and encouraged him to become more of a bully. They were altar boys together at church, but they also got into trouble together. One time, they cornered a kid and Henry was holding him down while John peed on him.

I panicked and took off running toward home as fast as I could. *If I don't get out of here, they could decide to hold me down and pee on me too!* I said to myself.

One day Bonnie and I were playing in the living room after going to church services at St. Anne's. We were roughhousing around a glass coffee table. While we were playing around, I pushed her into the coffee table. She hit it in such a way that glass shards went everywhere. She ended up needing stitches.

Mom and Dad were back together by the time we moved to a house with a big picture window—but they were never together for long. They would fight and break up, and then Mom would take us kids and move away from Dad. Then they would get back together again.

Throughout this period of time, Mom had begun shipping John to Daddy John's house. The thing was, Daddy John had started his own family soon after he and mom got divorced. So, when Mom sent my brother John his way, he sent John over to *his* mom's house (Grandma Lottie's). John would stay with Grandma until he got in trouble and ended up back with us. Or, until he threw a fit and said he wanted to come back. But while we were living in the picture-window house, he was with us most of the time.

Even though John gave me the occasional pounding, he was always my security blanket. We were family, and I overlooked his ornery ways. I liked having him around. We both had chores to do after school and we knew that we'd get our butts kicked if Dad came home and they weren't done. It was simpler to do our chores.

We would take turns being a lookout, keeping an eye on the big picture window in case Dad came pulling up. If one of us saw him come home, we'd sound the alarm, yelling, "Dad's home! Dad's home!"

One time, John and I were arguing over which of us was responsible for cleaning up a newspaper on the back porch which had been soiled by our puppy. We kept passing the buck back and forth, saying, "You do it! No, you do it!" We got to playing and it never did get done.

When Dad came home and realized that neither one of us had cleaned up the newspaper, he decided to upgrade our punishment. Instead of the usual whipping we got with the belt or his hand, he sent us into the backyard to pick a switch for our punishment.

I always chose the smallest one I could find. And John always chose a big one. After our beatings, I said to him, "You're so dumb! You should have picked a smaller switch!"

"No, *you're* so dumb!" he said. "The smaller ones do more damage."

Then we would turn around and show each other the wounds from our beating. My wounds all had little slits in the middle from the smaller switch.

Every time we were sent out into the yard to pick a switch for a beating, I made the same mistake, and every time, my brother let me.

SIX

WE SPENT THREE or four summers in a row at the home of Grandma Betty, Richard's mom. She and Grandpa lived within walking distance of downtown, in a big apartment above a barber shop. It was also across the street from a bar. When we were there, we stayed in their small spare room. I can't remember whether she told Mom that she wanted us kids there or I said I wanted to go. She was always nice to me and I knew that she loved me dearly.

Grandma was tall and thin with eyes that bulged just like Dad's. Grandpa Red, Dad's stepfather, stood seven feet tall. He was a gentle giant, kind, sweet and soft-spoken. Despite his size, he let Grandma feel like she was the boss.

You could set your watch by Grandma Betty and her routines. Every morning, she got up, went into the kitchen, cracked open an Old Milwaukee beer and lit a Pall Mall. I rarely saw her without a cigarette in her mouth and a beer in her hand. After Grandpa Red went off to work in the morning, Grandma spent half the day at the kitchen table, smoking and drinking.

I would go play for a little while and when I popped back into the kitchen, Grandma would still be sitting there. I don't remember her ever having the T.V. turned on but she often listened to swing music on the radio.

One of the things I liked most about being at their house was this tambourine-playing-monkey toy. I have no idea who it belonged to. All I know is that it made a terrible racket. Surprisingly, Grandma never made me shut it off or take it outside.

Dad ran numbers out of the bar across the street from Grandma's apartment, and one night, there was a big fight out in the hallway. Dad beat the daylights out of someone. Mom jumped in and swooped up us kids. Then she took us a few doors down the street to stay with her friend Ray and his wife, Boots, until things calmed down.

She laid us on blankets on the floor and then stayed up whispering with Boots half the night. The next morning when we woke up, John, Ricky and I were taken down the street and spent the day with Mom's sister, Aunt Peggy.

While I was there that day, I got into a tug-of-war over a golf club. My cousin Maria was standing at the top of an outdoor, two-story metal staircase. We each started pulling on opposite ends of the golf club.

"Fine!" she said. "Take it!" Then she let go.

I tumbled backwards down two flights of wrought-iron steps, landing at the bottom with my teeth protruding all the way through my lip. I was rushed to Mercy Hospital in Toledo—the same hospital where I was taken when I hit my head on the concrete overhang. A few stitches later, I was back at Aunt Peggy's.

My parents were ready to fix up another old house with an eye toward selling it. So, we moved into a Victorian fixer-upper. (I couldn't swear that we were still in Ohio, but I believe so.) The house sat on the corner in a cute little neighborhood. It was a two-story house with three upstairs bedrooms and plenty of space for us kids to run around.

The house didn't look very appealing when we first moved in, but it wasn't horrible either. Once Dad started working on it and turning it into a construction zone, there was a lot of yelling and cussing going on. I don't think my dad liked being a carpenter, but the work had to be done.

While we were living in this house, we had two dogs. My dad had brought home Mutley, the family dog, around the time that German Shepard bit my face. Now, Dad brought home Mutley's homeless brother, Brandy. They were both standard poodles—Mutley, white, and Brandy, a reddish-brown. The two dogs fought sometimes, just like human brothers.

One time while I was watching my little brother, Ricky, the two dogs got into a fight. When Ricky tried to break it up, he got bitten on his face. I ran him next door to the neighbors' house and they helped me call my mom. My parents came home and rushed Ricky to the hospital.

When I think back on this house, I see the loaded gun that sat on the bedside table in plain sight. Mom, meanwhile, kept a big butcher knife between the mattress and the box spring on her side of the bed. The presence of weapons in the house could be traced back to Fred and his threats to kill Mom. It didn't matter how much time passed, that dark cloud continued to loom over our family.

Fred wasn't the only threat my parents were guarding against. There were also the sketchy characters my dad dealt with on a daily basis. In his line of work, he had to collect money from people who had placed bad bets. There were also personal debts owed to him by people who lost to him at pool. The combination of losing and drinking made people ornery.

Between my dad's pool hustling, the threat of Fred returning, and my dad's shady jobs, my parents were understandably fearful and wanted to be armed. Given how often my parents fought, it was a miracle that neither of them picked up the gun or the butcher knife and killed the other. We kids were warned to stay out of my parents' bedroom, and away from the gun and the knife.

We were all sleeping one night when we heard a bunch of commotion from downstairs. A man was screaming, and the dogs were barking their heads off. Dad went running downstairs with his gun. Right behind him was Mom, running with her butcher knife. She slammed the boys' bedroom door and then slammed mine as she ran past.

When Dad got downstairs, he found our dogs Mutley and Brandy biting a drunken stranger. The guy had wandered into our house from the bar down the street. My parents never locked our doors. Dad pinned the man and held him there until the police arrived to pick him up. I found it exciting instead of scary.

While we were living in this house, I went to a new school. This one was within walking distance. John had his own set of friends who were older than me, and he liked to walk to school with them. He was ordered by Mom and Dad to wait for me in the morning and walk home with me after school. We rarely set out walking together. John always started out walking with his friends and then caught up with me at some point along the way.

As I walked towards home, an older boy who liked picking on me took it to a new level. He slammed my books out of my hands. I looked down at the ground to see my books scattered around. When I looked up again, I saw John on top of the guy. This wasn't the first time he had swooped in at the speed of lightning to save the day. He always appeared out of nowhere, like a comic-book superhero.

The kid had planned to bully me and then run off to safety. John gave him a real beating—and then my brother got suspended for fighting on school grounds. I never had any more kids picking on me after that.

John protected me and that felt good. Then, when we got home, he beat me up himself. Dad was like that too. Between being in prison and the military, he was very intimidating. But when I was little, I felt protected by him and felt like he loved me.

Dad would always say, "I'd take a bullet for you." He was always good to me and my brothers in those days and treated us like we were important to him.

It was like we had our own bodyguard. People would move out of Dad's way because he was an intimidating man. The fact that he was a sharp dresser made him even more intimidating. He usually wore a black leather blazer with dress pants. He looked like someone to be reckoned with, someone you'd step aside and let pass. Being quiet and shy, I felt good having an intimidating dad.

When I was in first grade, Dad bought me a diamond ring for my birthday. The ring was a little loose on my finger. The day after Dad gave it to me, I took it off so I could wash my hands. I set the ring on the counter by the sink. The counter was wet, and my ring slid down the drain. That was the last I saw of the ring. I was crushed, devastated. I couldn't stop crying.

As I got older, I became more and more aware of how much Mom and Dad fought. They went back and forth between being best friends and best enemies. I started to distrust my dad because I saw how mean he could be to my mom. She was a fighter and could give as good as she got, but that didn't excuse my dad's mistreatment of her. Not as far as I was concerned, anyway.

As I got older, I also started to wonder why Dad never adopted me. I wanted the same last name as everyone else in the house. (John had Daddy John's last name, just like I did.)

When I was younger, I assumed that it was because of the child-support money Mom was getting from Daddy John. I think my parents felt that if Mom had said to Daddy John, "Listen, Richard wants to adopt Suzette," the checks might have stopped coming.

When I got older, I wondered if maybe Mom also wanted to stick it to Daddy John. She was always mad at him. They didn't have a good breakup and were always arguing over the support payments.

SEVEN

DAD WAS WORKING at the Wonder Bread factory, making bread. At the end of the workday, he often brought home bread that didn't pass inspection. We never ate any bread other than Wonder Bread.

One day, Dad and his supervisor got into an argument over something and the supervisor took a swing at Dad.

In retaliation, Dad hauled off and hit his supervisor with a bread pan—and then filed a lawsuit against Wonder Bread. The fact that both Dad and the supervisor were union members factored into the lawsuit somehow. Dad won the lawsuit and received settlement money from Wonder Bread. Then he got a job working for Butler Manufacturing, making grain bins.

One night around this time, Mom woke me up by yanking me and my teddy bear out of bed. She and Dad had gotten into another one of their arguments. Mom was carrying Ricky in her arms and dragging me and my teddy bear down the hallway. (John must have been with Daddy John at the time.)

Mom got us all in the car and put it in gear. As Mom was trying to get away, Dad came running out of the house, and grabbed a shovel that was sitting by the door. He pole-vaulted the shovel through the rear window of the car.

Just in the nick of time, Mom shoved my head down into the seat, saving my life. Glass went flying everywhere and the shovel rested on the dashboard and the driver's seat.

Mom managed to skid out of the driveway, with me scared to death in the passenger seat. She took us to stay at Diane and Floyd's house. Diane had a little boy with an eye disability and an older daughter who looked after him. I understood how badly it must have felt for Diane and Floyd's boy to have eye problems. I had an eye patch after my eye surgery. We weren't there more than a couple of weeks before Mom and Dad got back together again.

Dad finalized his lawsuit with Wonder Bread and had his settlement money from them. He also fell and hurt his back at Butler Manufacturing, and had disability money coming in from them. His days of physical labor were over.

One day, Dad said to Mom, "Let's buy a business!"

They found a bar in Southaven, Minnesota and bought it on the spot. Then they packed up us kids and headed off down the road. I don't remember the drive—just the first place we lived. It was a long, narrow three-bedroom mobile home out in the country. It sat on the state highway, five miles from the bar my parents now owned.

Southaven had one streetlight running down the middle of the main street. My parents' bar was the bigger of the only two bars in town, and they featured bands with live music on the weekends.

Across the street from our mobile home was a set of railroad tracks that ran through town. Freight trains came by on a semi-regular schedule, but never passenger trains. When John and I got bored in our mobile home, we would go out by the tracks and wait for a freight train to come by going slowly enough for us to hop aboard.

We had learned to hop aboard trains when we lived on Auburn Street. The trains would pull up in front of the factory across the street. They were our playground and we loved to climb up and down their ladders. I was always hyperactive and impulsive, and John was a little bit calmer but not by much.

My brother was a good judge of how fast a train was going. Usually we hopped onto a train together while it was sitting idle. Or, if it was already moving, we managed to grab hold of the ladder that ran up the side of the train car. Often, he would still be pulling me onto the train the rest of the way as it started rolling. When the train stopped or slowed down to go through town, we hopped off and headed back home on foot.

One time, he managed to hop aboard a train while I was still calculating when to jump. I got left behind. I started running behind the train, trying to catch up. Our house was half a mile away.

As I ran alongside the train, John was reaching his hand out to me and yelling, "Come on!" Finally, he was able to grab my arm and help me onto the train.

By this point in my life, Dad's behavior toward me had taken a turn for the worse. It had started to shift during the final days we had spent in our previous house, before we went to Diane's. That's when he started becoming more and more aggressive. He started punishing me on a regular basis and becoming very loud.

Seeing Dad upset was always a little bit scary because I knew he kept a gun by his bed. I never forgot that he had been in prison for killing someone. Everyone knew that Dad was violent. He was the type of guy who might come and blow up your house while you were sleeping inside if he didn't like something you did or said.

On the one hand, I trusted that Mom would keep me safe. I also knew that my mom's family believed that it was Dad, not Fred, who had stabbed Mom. So, they didn't want Mom to be with Dad.

As I got older, I realized that the weapons kept around our house were probably meant for more than protection against Fred and the sketchy characters Dad dealt with in his crooked lines of work. Between the guns and knives and the fact that we moved so often, I figured out that Dad was on the run from the mob.

I overheard my parents talking about the fact that some of the guys my dad used to run numbers for were mobsters and they would come looking for him. Apparently, there was money that didn't get turned in. I found this totally believable because I knew that my dad was a dishonest person. There was no one he wouldn't scam. He was proud of who he was and had no shame. He didn't care what anyone thought of him.

One night not long after Mom and Dad bought the bar, they had finished cleaning and locking up, and got into their car to head home. It was around 3:00 in the morning and they were both very tired. Dad was in the passenger seat and our two dogs were in the back. Mom was driving when she fell asleep at the wheel.

Before she knew what was happening, the car was submerged in one of the many lakes in Minnesota. Mom was terrified and screaming that they were going to die. Dad was trying to pull Mom out of the car, and the dogs as well, but he was standing on the car to do it and that was pushing the car down even further. It was a miracle that they all made it out alive, even the dogs.

After the car accident, my parents decided to move closer to town so Mom wouldn't have to do as much driving. So, we moved to Moose Lake. Seeing the moose and deer outside in the woods, it was easy to see how the lake got its name.

Our trailer was deep in the woods, and there was nobody around for miles. There was a community of people out there but most of the time, they were out of sight. Then, when I least expected it, they would materialize before my eyes.

It was spooky. *Where did all these people come from?* I would wonder.

There was a one-lane road out to our trailer, with the surrounding trees clustered very close together—so it got eerie out there, especially at night. The silhouette of the moon shining through the trees would cast dark shadows. I was comforted by the nearness of the man in the moon. It helped me feel less scared of whatever might be lurking in the woods.

"Don't worry," John told me. "Just go to sleep and then in the morning, we will hop a train and go into town." Then he tucked Ricky into bed.

"Okay . . ." I said. I found John's words to be very calming and I was able to drift off to sleep.

I liked being on Moose Lake. I loved going ice skating with John when it was really cold. And, sometimes we went out on snowmobiles. Almost everyone there had a snowmobile. About fifty of us would get together to go snowmobiling on the lakes and party around big bonfires.

One day, Mom and I were following Dad back home—she and I on her Skidoo and Dad on his Scorpion. Mom's Skidoo was slower than Dad's Scorpion, and Mom was a bit of a scaredy-cat. So, she was going slower than Dad. By the time Mom and I went over this particular patch of ice, it must have been weakened due to Dad going over it first.

Mom and I hit a weak spot in the ice and our snowmobile began to sink down into the icy lake water. Dad slowed his snowmobile to a stop, hopped off, and managed to pull us off ours. He rescued us just in the nick of time. Dad couldn't save Mom's Skidoo but that was the second time his quick thinking had saved Mom from drowning.

Around this time, Aunt Peggy sent her son Eddie, who was a year younger than me, to live with us for a while. She wasn't very maternal and often sent her kids to stay with us. She had two children –Maria and Eddie—with her second husband. Her four oldest kids were still living with her first husband. Sometimes Maria also came to stay with us for big windows of time. She was two years older than me and close to John in age. She was like a big sister to me.

After a while, Aunt Peggy started coming to town a lot. She must have come to join her kids. Before too long, she got her own place on the outskirts of town in a rural area in a little trailer.

My parents had already moved Grandma Margaret into a trailer in town. Wherever we went, she went too. Mom liked to have her nearby to help with us kids.

When Grandma was watching us, I never knew which way things were going to swing. On the one hand, she was sweet. But if we got to fighting amongst ourselves, she would grab a spatula and chase us around the house. If she caught us, she gave us a spanking on our butts. When Marie and Eddie were with us, there were five of us underfoot, so she did a lot of chasing.

The spankings were the worst part of having Grandma watch us. The wonderful part about it was having her read to me. While Ricky was in bed in another room taking a nap, Grandma would sit up against some pillows, and read to me. She liked to read from the Bible, and I loved to hear her beautiful voice.

Grandma kept a little wooden keepsake box by her bed, filled with photos and other treasures. I would pull out a picture and say, "Grandma, what about this one? Tell me the story . . ."

"That's Art, who died on the power line," she said.

Or, I would pull out a piece of costume jewelry from the box and have her tell me the story behind it.

One day, Grandma and I were going through the trinket box and she was reading to me from the Bible. Suddenly, I saw smoke pouring from the room where Ricky was taking a nap.

"There's smoke!" I yelled, thinking that maybe Grandma had left a cigarette burning in there.

She ran down the hall with me right behind her. When we got into the room where Ricky had been sleeping, we found him in the middle of a burning bed. Grandma rushed in and scooped him up. She was yelling and horribly upset.

Meanwhile, Ricky was as happy as a pig in shit. He was standing on the bed in the middle of the flames. It turned out that my little brother had been playing with matches and set the bed on fire. He was only two years old and still really tiny, but he was fascinated by the fire.

Both Dad and Grandma were smokers, so it was no mystery as to where Ricky had gotten the matches. He had been napping in Mom and Dad's room where there were always matches laying around.

Grandma tried to put out the fire. Then, she got on the phone with Dad to get him to come home and help her. He was down at the bar, stocking the liquor, and had to run home. Thankfully, there was only a mile between Grandma's and the bar, so he got home in just a few minutes. He dragged the mattress outside and managed to beat the fire out of it.

I was surprised that Dad wasn't mad about the fire. There did seem to be some respect for the fact that we were the intruders in Grandma's house and one of our own had caught her bed on fire.

Another time, Grandma put Ricky down for a nap and then decided to lie down beside him for a little while as he slept. When she woke up, she and the bed were both on fire. Ricky had been playing with matches again. None of us were surprised when Ricky became interested in artillery when he went into the military. We were glad he finally found a way to put his skills to good use.

EIGHT

AFTER MOM AND Dad bought the bar, their relationship seemed a little fractured. They were arguing all the time. They weren't as focused on each other and seemed to have lost that playful, loving exchange they usually had between them. They worked different shifts and then got together to figure out the books. It was obvious that they were drifting apart.

They worked until very late at night down at the bar. Dad slept a lot during the daytime, but Mom only slept about four hours a night. Part of the reason for this was the fact that she was a night owl. The other factor was Dad, who thought nothing of getting her up in the middle of the night if he needed or wanted something. It seemed like she was always up and about, doing things around the house. She must have been completely sleep-deprived.

I would be in the middle of talking to her and she would start to fall asleep on her feet. I saw her eyes roll back in her head and thought to myself, *Oh, my God—she's dead!* I would shake her and start screaming but it would turn out that she was only taking a catnap. She never sat down; she just fell into a snooze while standing there having a conversation.

They got into an argument one day and Dad gave Mom a black eye. It was the first and only time he ever hit her. Much later in life, I found out from Mom that she had an affair with a man from the bar. It wasn't hard to see how this could have happened. While Dad was home sleeping during the day, Mom was usually working.

Sometimes Mom and Dad would let me follow them to the bar.

I loved cleaning the Co2 cannister which was used to make pop fizzy. It made a big whooshing sound, which I could trigger when cleaning the machine. I had a ball making those sounds.

I also got paid a few dollars by my parents for picking up things that had fallen onto the floor. I found all sorts of treasures on the floor of the bar—coins, dollar bills, fives. People would start drinking and pull money out of their pocket. Sometimes when they'd had a few, the money would slip from their hands onto the floor.

One time, I found the false teeth of a drunken guy. He was constantly losing his teeth. I got a five-dollar reward for finding them.

Sometimes there was money in the cigarette machine, and when I found a few coins, I got very excited. I would turn on the jukebox and have a party by myself. I'm sure anybody hearing the jukebox and peeking in the storefront would have been surprised. They would have seen no one inside the bar but a little girl, dancing around with a five-dollar-bill and false teeth in her hand.

The last time I found this man's false teeth, I said to my parents, "Let's surprise him and bring him his teeth!"

So, we showed up at his house. I reached out my tiny hand and gave him his teeth.

In return, he gave me a shiny new harmonica. It looked like a newer version of the big worn-out one he played for me that day. I had never heard anyone play the harmonica before that day and I loved the sound.

When I was around nine years old, we started to hire bands to come play music at the bar—usually polka music or country. I was allowed to go to the bar early before anyone was drunk, and listen to the music. Everyone would be dancing, singing and partying. I felt so proud because I was the one who had cleaned the bar.

One time, I took the train to the bar around eight o'clock in the morning. Mom was cleaning the place and doing the books. Since the bar was a community meeting place, they opened around 8:30 or 9:00 in the morning for those who wanted to come in and have breakfast.

I was bored, so I went out back to play. Next door to the bar was a butcher. All of a sudden, the doors to the butcher shop flew open. They were receiving a load of cattle or something. When the man who was making the delivery left, he didn't shut the door tight.

Oh, a door! I said to myself. *I've got to go in!*

As I went down a little hall, I heard the sounds of livestock. I went a little further and then I spotted a ladder leaning against the wall. I looked up and became curious about what was up there. I used the ladder to climb up into the loft of the barn. I used the beams to steady myself, and worked my way into the loft.

I watched the butcher pass by below. When I saw him lock the door, I wanted to shout, "Wait! Don't lock me in!" but I couldn't because I wasn't supposed to be in the rafters.

Down below, the butcher started to slaughter the animals. I could hear the gun going off as he shot them. Then I would hear the animals drop—a *bam!* from the shot and then a thud.

Oh, my God! I thought to myself. *I've got to get out of here!*

I waited until the man walked away. Then I snuck quietly down the wooden ladder and ran out of there. I felt sure that nobody saw me coming out of there, except my brother John.

Then my mom and dad came out the back door of the bar and joined me and John. Before we knew it, the man from the butcher shop had come outside.

"You all want to come in and see what goes on in here?" he asked. He seemed proud of his work as a butcher, but I thought that watching animals get slaughtered was disgusting.

Does he know I've just been inside? Is that why he's inviting us inside? I asked myself. I thought I'd been able to sneak out without being seen.

I quickly piped up, saying, "No, I'm good. No need for that!"

Money seemed to be an ongoing problem between Dad and other people. There was one lady in particular who stands out in my memory. Every once in a while, I would hear my mom talking about the woman.

Mom would yell at Dad, saying, "Why is this woman here?" Then the door would shut and I wouldn't get to hear the rest of the conversation.

My mother was very calm by nature and never one to be loud or upset. But whenever she talked about "this woman," she had a lot of attitude and a snippy tone in her voice. She wanted to know why this woman would come to the bar, sit at a table, and glare at my dad. She didn't understand why this was happening.

It came to light that Dad had borrowed thousands of dollars from the woman. And apparently, he hadn't paid back the money and wasn't planning to do so.

That was my dad—a con artist who could talk you out of your money. And this seemed to be one of those times. This woman came to the bar because Dad had something of hers and she wanted it repaid. Seeing that Dad wasn't taking his debt seriously, she was pissed.

Dad clearly enjoyed seeing her in that state. He could have told her to leave—and Mom wanted him to. "As far as I'm concerned, she could sit there all day," Dad said. He never did repay her.

Even at a very young age, I understood that Dad took advantage of people. If he was talking to someone and being nice, I became suspicious. I figured he was trying to borrow money or get over on them in some way. I would think to myself, *Little do they know, Dad's going to get them sooner or later!*

If we hadn't moved away, the woman probably would have kept after Dad for her money. Even after we left, she may have stalked Aunt Peggy, who took over the bar. If it hadn't been for Aunt Peggy, we never would have been able to leave.

Mom and Dad didn't leave the bar over that angry lady. They just left. Wanderlust again, no doubt.

When we first got to Minnesota, Dad was welding grain bins for Butler Manufacturing. One day, he was twenty-three feet up a ladder, welding, and fell. He seriously hurt himself. He sued Butler Manufacturing and got a settlement package. Miraculously, he didn't burn himself when he fell, even though he was welding at the time. But he hurt his back very badly, and it was never the same after that.

Since we were in Minnesota, Dad went to the Mayo Clinic for

surgery and spent a long time there. Mom was back and forth for some reason. I wasn't distressed not having Mom at home. I was used to it.

While Dad was in the Mayo Clinic, we stayed with Aunt Peggy in Minneapolis. We always had Aunt Peggy's kids with us so now it was Aunt Peggy's turn.

Meanwhile, we were now taking a school bus into a bigger town to go to a school that was brand new. The school was set up as a huge open gymnasium-type space, with the classes separated into pods. The pods were sectioned off with moveable dividers. There were no classrooms. There weren't even any walls.

I could vaguely hear the teacher in the class next to mine, but I couldn't really hear what she was saying. And I could hear people when they came in and out of the classroom. It made it impossible for me to concentrate. The other kids in class seemed to have no problem doing multiplication tables, but I couldn't remember the math.

We were supposed to be so happy to be going to this newly-built school but I found the setup to be a total nightmare. It would take some time for me to figure out that my problem was Attention Deficit Disorder (ADD). Back then, very few people had ever heard of ADD.

Mom kept getting called to school to talk about me, but no one could figure out what to do to help me. I underwent a lot of testing, including looking at ink blots.

"What do you see here?" they asked.

"I don't know. A butterfly?" Everything looked like a butterfly to me.

No one said to me, "You're having a hard time, so we want to give you these tests." They just shuffled me off to this one pod where they administered these tests. Meanwhile, all the other kids went off to class.

The testing seemed to go on forever. I spent at least two weeks sitting in a pod doing these tests. The tests started out simple and got harder from there. I was given both psychological testing and I.Q. testing. Finally, they figured out that I had ADD and made a plan for me to slow down and move to a quieter room. That helped me a little bit.

Later when I became a working adult, a psychiatrist told me, "The injury to the frontal lobe of your brain you sustained as a kid was probably giving you blocks. That's what was making it hard to do math.

I wouldn't worry, though. I don't know *anyone* who manages to do all the things you do in the course of your life! You have run your own hair salons, owned other businesses and taken care of your family."

I never let the brain damage from my injury bother me. I believed Mom when she would say to me, "Don't worry about all that. Look at all the good things!"

Once Dad got out of the Mayo Clinic, he and Mom decided that we should move to Florida for the warm weather. I'm not sure what the weather had to do with Dad's injured back. Maybe he got an aching in his bones when it was cold outside, just like I do now.

NINE

WE MOVED FROM Southaven, Minnesota where the bar was located to Palm Harbor. Florida. I wasn't sure how this move was going to work out because it was so obvious that things between Mom and Dad were seriously strained.

I didn't find out until later what had caused the strain between my parents. Here's what happened. There was a man who was killed when his car collided with a train. The train tracks were only a few buildings from the bar. It was rumored that Dad had pushed the man's car onto the train tracks.

I said to myself, *But if this man died in his car on the railroad tracks, how could Dad have been behind that? Those are just wicked rumors about Dad.*

Then it came to light that the man who was killed was the same man who'd had an affair with Mom. And it was rumored that Dad had been in his car, waiting behind the guy's car, and pushed the guy's car onto the tracks.

I said to myself, *Well, Dad's pretty wicked. He's killed people before. He's perfectly capable of doing it again.*

I remembered Dad saying to me, "Your mom brought you into this world. I can take you out."

A few months after the man died on the railroad tracks, there were two other car accidents. In one accident, the parents of one of my classmates died. Then a car full of six teenage kids got into a car accident. The kids were all from our school and every last one of them died.

I don't remember what the teenage kids crashed into. I do know that alcohol was involved—and our bar was one of only two establishments in town that sold alcohol. Rumors were that the teens either got beer from the liquor store across the street, or from our bar. The deaths of these teenagers really affected me. I didn't go to the funeral of the teens, but I went with some other kids from my school to the joint funeral of the parents of our classmate.

We all got out of class and rode the school bus to the funeral. We were ordered off the bus and herded into the church like cattle. Then we were guided up the aisle and past the open caskets of the adults who had died. That was my first sighting of dead people and I thought I might pass out.

As I sat with my group from the bus, they were all crying. I wanted out of there really badly. It was the first time I ever noticed how anxious I got in crowds.

I had high hopes for our new location, and hoped it would repair my parents' fractured relationship. That's how we did things in our family. There was an unspoken understanding that we would leave behind our troubles and start over in a brand-new place, with brand-new furniture. I was excited for the new journey. I loved the unknown, the newness, and the adventure of it all.

We moved so often, it never seemed strange to me. Sometimes I would come home, things would be packed, and Mom and Dad would say, "Get in the car. We're moving."

Sometimes we would pack for weeks before a move and sometimes we would leave behind all our belongings, except for our clothes. Even when we did pack our belongings and take them with us, we always left the furniture behind. Dad liked to buy new furniture to decorate a new place.

It was cold when we left Minnesota for the long drive to Florida. Dad had a big El Dorado Cadillac convertible and a Volkswagen. I was in the Volkswagen with Mom while Dad was driving the Cadillac.

I was so glad I was in the car Mom was driving. Whenever I was in the same car as Dad on a family car ride, I was absolutely miserable. Dad was a chain smoker. He would smoke one right after another with the windows rolled all the way up. The car would fill with smoke and the smell of it disgusted me. I would fake cough until Mom finally rolled her windows down.

When we arrived at our new location, we pulled into a driveway. Suddenly, I saw trailer after trailer after trailer. We had lived in a trailer on Moose Lake in Minnesota but I had never seen or lived in an entire *community* of trailers before. I didn't even know that trailer parks existed.

This was our new home: a corner lot at Dunedin's Lone Pine Trailer Park. It felt like we were driving onto a gameboard. All the lawns were perfect, all the trees were symmetrically placed, and there were flowers everywhere. It was green and lush and the most beautiful sight I had ever seen. I was so happy to be there.

When we made this move to Florida, we took only our clothes and what we needed to get by. Our new trailer home was beautiful—nice and clean. It was a three-bedroom place.

When we first got there, my brother John was staying with Daddy John. It was a few weeks before he joined us. Whenever John did something wrong and the police were looking for him, my parents would send him to live with Grandma or Daddy John for a little while. So, he was often back and forth between Daddy John's place and Mom and Dad's.

Since John wasn't always with us, when he did join us, we had to figure out where to put him. He ended up sharing Ricky's room but spent a lot of time on the screened-in porch. He always liked to find his own spot wherever we were at. During the day, he would take his guitar out onto the porch and get into his zone. And at night, he sometimes slept on a couch out there.

I don't remember a lot about the town of Dunedin where the trailer park was located. The park itself was rural and about seven miles from The Countryside Mall. It was kind of off the beaten path. A main road ran through the trailer park and seemed to go on forever. Quite a distance from our trailer, on one side of that main road, was a cemetery up on a hill. Even the cemetery was beautiful in my eyes. I loved its lush green lawn.

When we lived in Detroit, we had to be real careful going outside. Then, when we lived in Minnesota, we were so far out in the country, there was no one to play with me. So, I was constantly getting into fights with my brother John.

In the trailer park where we lived, life was less dangerous, so I had more freedom to spend time outside. I met some of the neighbor kids and made more and more friends over time. This was the first time I really had the luxury of saying, "I'm going outside to play with my friends."

One family in the trailer park had two kids—a little girl named Barbie and her brother, redheaded Johnny. I fell in love with him. During the time we were living in Minnesota and staying with Grandma, I'd had a little redheaded friend named Mary Ellen. My grandma always hated anyone with red hair. She told me that I couldn't have Mary Ellen at my house. She made me think that redheads were bad.

Any time Johnny smiled at me, I could see his one silver tooth. It shone like a diamond. I thought he was so cute, and his silver tooth was the most beautiful thing I'd ever seen. I got weak in the knees any time he smiled at me. The fact that he rode motocross and knew how to do jumps made him even more exciting to me.

In order to be around Johnny, I found excuses to go and play with his little sister, Barbie. Johnny and Barbie's family lived at the other end of the trailer park. I would finish my chores as fast as I could and then run all the way down to their house.

Everything changed when my dad got wind of the fact that I was going down the street to see a boy. Someone had seen me walking and talking with Johnny and Barbie and told my dad. Then he started calling me a dirty, nasty whore and saying that I wasn't allowed to go outside anymore unless I stayed within his line of sight.

It was true that I was dressing more like a girl now in hopes of getting Johnny to notice me, but I was still ladylike. I wanted to say to my dad, *I know what whore means, thank you very much. Why don't you just stab me in the face if you're going to call me that?*

One of my friends at the trailer park was a girl named Robin. She was older than me, real tall, and had a big scar which ran from one side of her face to the other. She had gotten the scar thanks to a run-in with a barbed wire fence between the cemetery and the trailer park.

Robin lived like she had no parents. Her mom was a waitress who went straight into her bedroom when she got off work. She always had pill bottles piled up on her nightstand. When I looked at her lying in her bed, she looked thin and unhealthy. I never saw Robin's father at all.

Since Robin's mom was technically home even when she was locked away in her room by herself, my parents were fine with me going over there. "Sure, you can go over to Robin's," they would say.

Robin and I would listen to music on the radio, and sometimes we called the radio stations and made requests for them to play certain songs. One time when we got a little older, we snuck out late at night. We pushed the car down the driveway so Robin's mom wouldn't hear us starting it, and then hopped in and turned the key in the ignition.

While Robin's mom lay in her bed, drugged out, we took her Dodge Dart for a joy ride. We zoomed around the trailer park, laughing all the way. Then we left the trailer park, drove into the cemetery and went all the way to the end. The car stopped abruptly for some reason and there we were, stuck in the cemetery in the dark. Somehow Robin got the car running again, and we made our way back to her house. We snuck into our houses and nobody was ever the wiser.

From that point on, Robin got into the habit of yelling at her mom and throwing things at her. I couldn't imagine being mean to my own sweet, kind, loving mom. I didn't understand why Robin was being so mean to her mom. I said to myself, *Maybe Robin just needs attention.*

I started out envying her all the freedoms she had. Then, I realized that having no one to tell you anything about life or give you any attention at all was worse than having my parents tell me what to do.

Then there were the neighbors directly across the street from us and a few doors down. The husband in the family, Greg, had suffered from polio as a kid and couldn't get around without crutches.

One Fourth of July, my dad and Greg drove all the way from Florida to Tennessee and Georgia to buy fireworks. They filled up the car and then drove back. Dad said they spent $800. We hauled their huge load of fireworks down to the beach.

As the sun set over the ocean, the adults were getting drunk and laughing. All of us kids went into the ocean to play. Greg made a fireworks display so powerful, it sounded like bombs going off.

Mom and Dad spent a lot of time with two couples—Kathy and her husband and Greg and his wife. At some point while we were living there, the two couples got divorced and remarried each other. I thought it was the strangest thing.

At first, our social circle survived the restructuring. Before long, though, the dynamic started to shift, and the friendships became fractured. After a while, nothing was the same. Without that social circle, the entire experience of living there changed and my parents started thinking about moving again.

Greg became Dad's best friend and a mentor to me. Until I met Greg, I was afraid of swimming. All my life, I had told myself what I had heard all the other women in our family say: *The women in our family don't swim!* All the female influencers in my life were non-swimmers—my mom, Grandma, Aunt Peggy, Aunt Sunny.

Then Greg taught me how to swim. He didn't sit down and say to me, "This is how you swim" and explain to me the ins and outs of swimming. He showed me. My aunt had a pool at her place, so we went over there and he jumped in the pool.

It was shocking to see this guy who couldn't walk take a seat on the edge of the pool and fearlessly jump in. It turned out that his upper body was very strong. He had developed it to compensate for the paralysis in his legs. He didn't let anything stop him, and he was a great example of overcoming obstacles.

Greg nicknamed me Cinderella. Being Dad's best friend, Greg knew that Dad had me do a lot of the household chores. I had to stand on a chair to do the dishes. If, God forbid, I missed a spot, Dad made me re-wash not only the dirty dishes but all the dishes in the cupboard.

Sometimes, Dad would see something someone left sitting on the floor and say, "That damned thing has been sitting on the floor so long, I walked over it a hundred times! Why won't you pick it up?"

I wanted to say, *Why do I have to do everything? If you walked over it a hundred times, why didn't you just pick it up yourself?*

I couldn't understand why my dad wouldn't do anything to help me. My mother would try to help me with my chores when Dad wasn't around. Or, if I was doing chores and I missed something, Mom would secretly try to help me before Dad found my mistake. When he *was* around, she was Dad's queen. He wouldn't hear of her doing chores—unless, of course, they involved cooking for him and catering to him.

Dad would ask me, "Did you finish your chores?"

If I said yes, he would take his finger and do a dust test along the top of the stereo. Then he would take a Q-tip and check to see if I got all the dust out from the wooden scrollwork on the stereo cabinet.

"You didn't get in here!" he would say. Then he would make me sit with the Old Gold and meticulously clean every crevice.

He would often tell me, "Get this done before you go anywhere!"

If I didn't do what I was supposed to do, I would get in big trouble. Dad would give me a beating and sometimes I would get grounded. I didn't like the treatment I got from him, but I didn't really think anything of it. It was just my life.

TEN

ONE TIME, DAD told me that I couldn't go anywhere until I vacuumed our front porch which was covered in indoor-outdoor carpeting. Dad was all about the clean. I went to the closet and took out the shiny, new silver Electrolux that Dad had bought for three hundred dollars. I accidentally sucked up all the rain water on the front porch and broke the motor in the brand-new vacuum cleaner.

I was beaten real badly over that incident. It was the first time I remember getting a bad beating as a big girl. Part of me had always felt like I deserved the beatings. Maybe I was mouthy and sassed off, or didn't do my chores right, or maybe I overloaded the dryer.

Another part of me felt like, *I don't know how I'm expected to know all these things! Why is he beating me over this stuff? And does this beating really have to go on for so long?*

It didn't seem right that I would get beaten over doing my chores wrong. I felt like Dad was the one who should have taught me the right way to do them. The worst part was, whenever Dad wanted to give me a beating with the belt, he made me go pick out the belt.

I would stand there and think to myself, *The big one? The small one? Which one will hurt less?* The only thing I knew for sure was that I needed to pick a belt with no buckle.

Sometimes Dad beat me with a switch from a tree in the backyard—like that time I told you about when John and I failed to clean up the puppy poop on the newspapers.

Part of me naturally wanted to defend myself. But I was always a little bitty thing. Then, as I got older and bigger, I was better able to run away. If I tried to fight back, Dad would try to grab me by the arm and yank me down over a chair so I would stay put for the rest of the whipping.

When I saw Dad coming at me with the belt, I would say, "You're not gonna hit me!" And I would put my hands up in front of my face.

By the time I was nine or ten years old, I knew that these beatings were wrong—especially when I was getting beaten over something I had done on accident. I said to myself, *Enough is enough!*

One evening around the Fourth of July, we were making our way home long after dark, with Dad behind the wheel. Ricky and I were in the backseat, and we may have had one of our little friends with us.

Dad did something that caught the attention of a law enforcement officer driving by. Our drive home quickly turned into something out of a cop show. Dad decided that his best move was to try to escape the policeman, and he started speeding down some side streets.

"Keep your heads down!" he yelled.

As Dad jerked the steering wheel from left to right, we got whipped around in the backseat and kept sliding from one side window to the other. Finally, he pulled into a random driveway, shut off the car and killed the lights.

"Shut up and don't anybody talk!" he ordered.

We sat there dazed, not saying a word, for about half an hour. Then Dad quietly started up the car and slowly took us home the back way. None of us ever mentioned it again.

That was my dad. He was probably buzzed, hoping to avoid a ticket, and wanted to see if he could outrun the cops. That incident was an average night out on the weekend for him.

My last meaningful memory at the trailer park took place on Halloween. Mom liked to sew, and often made clothes for me. This Halloween, she made me a genie costume, fashioned after Barbara Eden's outfit in *I Dream of Jeannie*. The costume had Jeannie's harem pants and the little matching top she always wore on the T.V. show.

We always liked to trick-or-treat in Spanish Trails where the rich people lived. But this Halloween night, I was tripping over the puffy legs on my costume and falling down. Suddenly, the rich people's houses seemed really far apart, and it took forever to go from house to house.

This is so stupid! I was thinking. *I'd rather go to a neighborhood with a shorter distance between houses.*

After being out drinking one night at the Horseshoe Bar, my parents started fighting. They carried the argument into the trailer with them. I half awoke to hear loud talking but I didn't pay much attention to it. I thought to myself, *What else is new?*

The next thing I knew, Mom was pulling on the arm of my pajamas to get me to wake up, and saying, "Come on! It's time to go."

Ricky's legs were already wrapped around her and he was sleeping on her shoulder.

When I got out of my bedroom, I could see bright police lights shining into our dimly lit trailer. I also heard voices booming from a megaphone outside.

"Come out slowly!" said a loud voice. At first, the police seemed to simply be trying to get my dad to come out. But, he was staying put, so Mom figured she had better get us out.

In order to follow the megaphone sound coming from our front yard and get out the door, we had to pass by Dad. We walked sideways past him, one slow step at a time, as he sat in a chair with a shotgun across his lap.

I had never seen him look quite so scary. His brown eyes were fixed and dilated, almost black, as he stared off into nothing. Looking at his face, I thought, *It's like he's not even in there!*

There was no way of knowing who had called the police, but we figured it was probably the neighbors. They must have heard Mom and Dad arguing. Mobile homes have notoriously thin walls.

I didn't understand why Mom was having us walk right by Dad. He was sitting there with a shotgun in his lap. He could have easily reached out and grabbed us and killed us. I always believed that in his heart of hearts, he really did love us. That must have been why he let us pass by without hurting us.

When we got out front, the police instructed us to go across the street and wait. As we stood there, I saw the police removing Dad from our trailer.

As Dad came out, he was pushing the officers and trying to wrestle them off of him. Meanwhile, they were grabbing him and trying to maintain their grip. Dad managed to push one of the cops right into the garbage can which sat in front of our place. He landed butt-first, with his legs sticking out of the can.

(That officer was known in our neighborhood as Scarface. When I was sixteen or seventeen, I would end up in a driver's class being led by him. When I saw him up at the front of the class, I panicked, thinking he would remember me. Luckily, my face didn't seem to ring any bells for him. His face wasn't so easy to forget, with that big scar on it.)

When Dad pushed the police officer into the trash can, it triggered the arrival of even more police. They showed up, guns drawn, and Dad was hauled away in a police car. It turned out to be exactly as we figured: the neighbors had called in a domestic violence call because of the fighting they heard coming from our place.

When I was about ten or eleven years old, we moved into brand-new apartments in Palm Harbor, the town where we'd lived in the trailer park. By the time we moved, Kathy's family had broken up and sold their trailer. So, they asked us if we would keep their daughter's bedroom set until they were settled and could come back for it.

It was my very first matching bedroom set—white with a mirror over the dresser. It was the prettiest thing I'd ever seen. (When the family later came to take it back from me, I thought I was going to die.)

Right before we moved into the new apartments, I asked my mother, "Why are we leaving the trailer park, Mom? It's great here!"

"You know the cemetery we pass every day on our way in and out of the park? Well, it upsets your dad."

"But, why? Is it because of all the dead people in there?"

"Not exactly. Having to drive by the cemetery three or four times every day brought back all those tragic memories. It really ate him up," said Mom.

"What memories?" I didn't know what she was talking about. This was the first time I was hearing of this.

"Well, you know how Richard and his half-brother were playing in the cemetery when they were young? And remember how I told you his half-brother died when a gravestone got loose and fell on him?"

"I don't remember you telling me. That's really sad," I said.

When Richard's half-brother was killed by the gravestone in the cemetery, and Richard was sent to live in the orphanage, that marked the end of Richard having his family. He and his mother stayed in touch a little bit—but they only reunited later in life, once he'd gotten out of prison.

Now that I had the whole story, I felt badly for my dad. I realized he'd been through more than I ever knew. It made me feel better about having to move from the trailer park. I totally understood why it was best for us to get out of there.

This talk also made me feel good for another reason. I thought to myself, *Now that I'm getting older, Mom can really talk to me about things.*

Dad had been taking prescription medication for his back injury and doing binge drinking on the weekends. The drugs and the alcohol combined with his traumatic memories. This made Dad more ornery than usual. He was treating me badly and calling me a whore for playing with the kids down the street.

Meanwhile, my brother John was still being shuffled back and forth between our house and Daddy John's. He would be with us, and then not be with us, and then come back again. He was always in and out and sometimes in trouble. Sometimes he would fight to the death over absolutely nothing.

At those times, I would say to myself, *John doesn't seem like himself right now.*

Being shuffled back and forth between the two households was hard on him. He lived with a certain amount of emotional pain over it.

John was spending more time with us than he was with Daddy John. When he was with us, he spent a lot of time in his room. He had wall-to-wall black fur covering the walls. He had a black light and posters to go with the black fur. I thought it was the coolest room I'd ever seen.

ELEVEN

I WAS ASSIGNED THE role of school-bus patrol person, and given a belt and a badge to wear. I was put in charge of telling everyone on the school bus to sit down and be quiet. I'm not sure how I ended up on bus patrol but it may have simply been my turn.

One day, one of the kids on the bus refused to sit down. I stuck my knee in his stomach until he doubled over. Then I gave him a good hard punch in the face until he got a nosebleed. I tore him up.

Between the fights I got into with my brother John and the whippings I got from my dad, I was tough. I had never been in a position of authority before and I did what came naturally. I had learned growing up in my household that this was how you handled people.

I was determined to get the kid to sit down but then I was the one who was made to sit down. Yet, the bus driver didn't seem mad at me at all. I probably did what the bus driver dreamed of doing.

On my way off the bus, the driver said in a matter-of-fact tone of voice, "I'll take your badge now." I was immediately dismissed from my duties, but I got no further punishment. Nobody even asked me about the incident.

On the weekends, Dad made me deep-clean the house. By Sundays, I'd had enough of it. So, I had the bus from the local Baptist Church come pick me up and take me to services. I was actually Catholic, but I needed to get out of the deep-cleaning chores, and the Baptists had their own bus.

Grandma Margaret went to church and lived with us when we were little. She had instilled in me the importance of Sunday services. Thanks to my grandmother and her faith, I was given a solid foundation. I genuinely loved going to church for a whole bunch of reasons—getting out of the house, using part of the donation money for bowling, and getting saved. No one else in my family attended services.

Every Sunday during church services, I got saved all over again. I waved my arms and sang with my eyes closed. It always felt to me like the walls were shaking. The pastor was always trying to get the Holy Spirit into me by pushing on my forehead. He seemed to think he could drive the Holy Spirit right into my head.

The getting-saved part of the service came about forty-five minutes before services were over. I'd already been saved over and over, so sometimes I slipped out early and headed to the bowling alley. I would get in a little bit of bowling, keeping one eye on the clock. Then I'd race back over to church in time to board the church bus that would take me back home.

My parents moved us into an apartment on Highland Avenue in Dunedin, right next door to the apartment where silver-toothed Johnny lived with his sister, Barbie.

I was in heaven having Johnny next door, and wondered, *How did I get so lucky?* The only thing I could figure was that my mom had stayed in touch with the kids' mom. In any case, it was great having playmates next door. Danny, a guy who was friends with my brother John when we lived at the trailer park, also lived in the complex.

Our new home was a three-bedroom apartment with a big beautiful pool right off to the side of our back door. There was also an on-site laundry room, which meant we no longer had to load up the car and drive to the laundromat.

Dad and Mom seemed really happy in our new place. They had fun shopping for new furniture and decorating the apartment. Every single time we moved to a new place, my parents would leave the old furniture behind. But they usually brought our beds along.

I had attended Dunedin Elementary School before we moved. Now, I was going to Dunedin Junior High, which was an easy walk from our complex. I went to school without any real goals in mind. My parents had never spoken to me about college or what I might want to be when I grew up. They had their hands full, just living day to day.

I think the concern was over my abilities. Nobody wanted me to dream real big. Mom would always say, "If you tried your hardest, you've done your best." I don't think they expected too much of me. It didn't make me feel badly. I just thought it was my mom being sweet, as always.

I already knew what I wanted to be—a hairdresser, just like Grandma Margaret, who was already a hairdresser, and Mom, who had been in beauty school when she was pregnant with me.

At night, I would sneak out and go to the park to play post office. Our house was on the main floor and so was Johnny and Barbie's. We would pop out our windows and wave our arms when we were ready to go. That way, none of us would be out there alone.

We weren't in that apartment long before Mom got a call from Diane, the wife of Floyd, my dad's best friend from prison. Floyd had a friend who needed a place to stay. We had stayed with Floyd and Diane earlier in my life, so my parents may have felt like they owed them. In any case, this friend of Floyd and Diane's, along with his wife and their two kids, came to stay with us.

The parents and their son took John's room, which was empty at the time because he was at Daddy John's. The daughter, who was a couple of years older than me, stayed in my room with me.

One night, we snuck out the window and went down to the park to swim with the other neighborhood kids.

"We're going skinny-dipping," she announced, taking off all her clothes and jumping into the pool without me.

"No, we're not!" I said, without even knowing the meaning of the word. I saw her taking her clothes off and that was all I needed to know.

She was in the pool only about five minutes before I wanted to get her out and get her dressed again. "Come on, it's time to go! It's time to go!" I said, trying to get her to put her clothes back on.

When she climbed out of the pool, she put on her clothes and then stepped on a hunk of broken glass. It almost took her foot off. I had never seen so much blood in my life. She started to scream from the pain.

"Shh!" I said, hushing her. "You'll wake everyone up!"

I had her drape her arm around me. Then, with my help, we hobbled back to the apartment. We went as fast as we could under the circumstances, with her leaving a big trail of blood behind her as she went along.

She kept screaming and I kept trying to get her to keep quiet. As we got close to our apartment, all the inside lights suddenly came on in our unit. I had assumed our parents would have been asleep by that time. They were actually in the living room, watching T.V.

"Suzette Renee! You get to your room right now . . . and stay there!" said my dad in a very stern voice. Any time my parents used my middle name, I knew I was in serious trouble.

It turned out that she had hit an artery when she stepped on the hunk of glass. My dad wrapped her foot while we all waited for the ambulance to arrive. I stayed in my room while the rest of them got in the car and followed the ambulance to the hospital.

I knew I would be grounded for a while. That was nothing new. I was always grounded.

Dad would say, "The belt or restriction. It's your choice."

Choosing the belt meant that I was going to get my ass whipped. As I got older, I always chose restriction, and when I wanted to go out while I was on restriction, I snuck out.

Having this family staying with us added an extra layer of chaos to our already chaotic household. I thought it was fun having them there—but it didn't take more than a couple of weeks for it to start to wear on my parents.

One day not long after the broken-glass incident, the family was out running errands or something. I heard Dad say to Mom, "This place is too small. We can't keep helping these people! They're not doing anything to help themselves and she's got a drug problem . . ."

I had noticed that the mother seemed to sleep all the time. Until I heard Dad say that, I hadn't put two and two together.

The father was doing the best he could but he seemed more like the mother to me. He and the mother had switched roles. He was doing all the mom stuff she should have been doing. Maybe it was because she was always drugged out and sleeping. Not long afterward, they moved back to their home in Ohio.

My neighbor friends, Johnny and Barbie, and I were just across the hall. We ran back and forth to each other's apartments on a daily basis. There were only four units in the entire building, and we had the entire downstairs.

I got my first kiss in that building. I snuck out to play hide-and-seek while I was on restriction. Barbie was counting with her eyes closed at the time. Johnny had run ahead of me to the other side of the apartment and I didn't know where he went. I ran into a closet to hide, shutting the accordion doors behind me.

Suddenly, Johnny popped out of a clothes basket. He stood really close to me and was a little taller than I. As I looked into his blue eyes, a ray of sunlight shone through the slats in the door and sparkled off his silver front tooth. He had one arm on the side wall. He put the other arm around me, pulled me close, and gave me a big kiss. From that moment on, we had an unspoken agreement that he was my boyfriend.

We would all meet up at the laundromat in the apartment complex. My friends would really destroy the place. They moved the washing machines, tried to get the quarters out of them, and messed with the boxes of soap. I always felt badly about it and refused to participate. I even stayed behind to clean it up. I always worried that I would get caught cleaning the laundromat and be blamed for the vandalism.

Meanwhile, my brother John was taking karate classes and I was the holder of the pillow he used to practice his karate kicks. Every time he would kick the pillow I was holding, he would knock me to the ground. I was as light as a feather. As John got better and better at karate, I started to get really scared of being his pillow holder.

I would stay outside or get in the pool or do anything I could think of to avoid him. They had two pools in the complex and I became a good swimmer while we lived there. I loved being in the pool. I would listen for the sounds of his guitar coming from his room and think to myself, *Okay, good . . . now I know he's in his room, so he won't want me to hold the pillow. I'm going swimming!*

While we were living in that building, Dad drove me to school in his big, gold convertible El Dorado. As a fifth or sixth grader at the time, I was so embarrassed to have my dad pull up in front of the school in his huge Cadillac.

We only lived there for eight months or so, including the summer months. That's when I got to spend time with friend Darla. She was being raised by a single mom who was a hairdresser. They lived in a cute house that was beautifully decorated. They even had their very own pool in the backyard.

Darla's mom had a little salon in the house. I already knew I wanted to be a hairdresser but I had never thought of doing people's hair in my house. Suddenly, I realized, *Wait a minute, a single woman can have her own house, a pool, and a home salon? This is for me! I want this someday.*

This was the first time I started to understand household finances and the way rich people handled their money. People like us didn't have money; we just got by from day to day.

After I saw Darla's mom's home-based salon, I went and talked to Grandma about becoming a hairdresser. "Remember, Suzy, if you're a hairdresser, you will always be able to make ends meet and feed your family." (When I was little, everyone called me Suzy. To this day, my brothers John and Ricky still call me Suzy.)

We lived there through the fall and winter months and celebrated Christmas and New Year's there. When Christmastime came, we had a beautiful tree. The entire apartment was decked out. On Christmas morning, there were so many presents under the tree, I couldn't believe it. They just kept on coming. It was the first year my parents had credit cards. It wouldn't be long before the phone started ringing off the hook with creditors wanting their bills paid.

We all sat around the kitchen table, playing the Monopoly game that Santa brought us that year. Dad always took charge as the banker and enjoyed every minute of it. He was sneaky, hiding money and cards under the table. It was rare to see Dad really enjoying himself with us kids. That Christmas, he was really happy and spoiled us rotten.

We tuned into Dick Clark's New Year's Eve show on T.V. to watch the ball drop. I also watched the *Sonny & Cher* show with my dad. We were both big T.V. fans and watching it together gave us a pastime we could share without arguing.

At the end of the Christmas break from school, we got a call. The mom in the family that had been staying with us—the one who took drugs and slept all day—had taken too many of her pills and died of an overdose.

I felt really badly when I heard the news. At the dinner table, we all said a prayer for the family. I thought about all the time she had spent in a dark room in our house, sleeping. I wondered whether or not she had overdosed on purpose. I worried about the kids not having their mom and thought about me still having an awesome mom. Then I realized that their mom hadn't really been there for them anyway. At least they still had their dad and he already functioned as their mom, as far as I could tell.

I knew how the other family must have felt because I had already experienced a death in our family. When we were living in Toledo, Grandma Tuttle (Aunt Ethel's mother) had passed away. I don't think Mom even told us about Grandma's death. She just took off down the street, with me chasing her. When I got back to the house, whoever was watching us kids at the time told us that Grandma had died. Mom had gone to do her hair for the funeral.

One day, I opened our apartment door to leave for school, and found a big white piece of paper taped to the door. It was taped on very securely, so I left it there for my parents to read later. I knew it wasn't anything good.

When I got home from school that day, I found Mom and Dad taping up the last of the boxes. We were getting ready to move again. My parents hadn't paid the rent and weren't surprised to get the eviction notice.

It wasn't so much that they didn't *have* the money to pay the rent. Between Dad's various checks, he was bringing in about three thousand dollars a month. That was decent money back then. The problem was, they had overspent on Christmas, and there wasn't enough money left over for necessities like rent.

Sometimes they wouldn't pay the rent, knowing it would take a couple of months for a landlord to evict us. That was all the time Mom and Dad needed to save the money to get our next house.

When we left, Mom and Dad sneaked boxes of our belongings out at night. Otherwise, they would have run the risk of the landlord locking us out and keeping all of our things.

TWELVE

W HEN I WAS in sixth grade, Mom and Dad bought a mobile home in a trailer park off U.S. Highway 19 in Palm Harbor. When we pulled up to the mobile home for the first time, it was late at night. I had never seen the place in daylight. I ran in the back door and quickly scoped out the bedrooms. The rule among us kids was that whoever got there first got to choose their room. We all understood that the biggest room was Mom and Dad's and the rest were up for grabs.

It was only a three-bedroom place, so my choices were limited. After dismissing the room my parents would want, I raced into the first of the other two bedrooms and flipped on the light. Then I opened the closet door—and a flying palmetto bug flew out and landed in my hair, which was very long.

I spun around, screaming, and wildly batting at my hair with my hands. The bug burrowed deeper into my hair, making an awful hissing sound. This wasn't my first rodeo—I had seen the same bugs all over Florida. But it was the first time one ever landed in my hair.

I chose that room anyway because it was the biggest and best of the two. But there was no way I could sleep in there that night. I decided to sleep on the couch in the living room in case the bug had any brothers and sisters. Thankfully, after thoroughly dousing the place with bug spray, I never saw another bug in there.

My brother John was spending more time with us during this period, and less time with Daddy John, so he and Ricky shared a room. John was a pacer. So, during those times when he was staying at our house,

I would often wake up at four in the morning because I heard him pacing back and forth.

He was in his early teens when he came to me and showed me a little "42" tattoo on his arm. "I'm in a gang now," he said. I wasn't sure whether 42 was the gang's name or what.

John was also getting into fights at school, so there were times when he was in trouble with the police. On top of the fights, there were the mischievous things he did at school, like the time he blew up the toilet in the boys' bathroom.

Whenever the cops were out looking for my brother, Mom would call up Daddy John and say, "You'd better take him quick! The police are after him."

Whenever Dad was being mean to me, as he often was, I would lie in bed at night, crying. And I would wonder what Daddy John looked and smelled like.

I would say to myself, *If my real father was here, I wonder if he would save me from this. Why doesn't he care about me, or claim me as his?*

Around our trailer were four or five other trailers. We all got to know each other and formed a little neighbor network. We would spend time at each other's houses, or on each other's porches. The adults would sit around in the evenings and drink beer together.

Our neighbors Buzzy and Diane were about twenty-six and childless. There was also the Woods family, living to the right of us and two trailers down. They were a big family with five or six kids. They had a boy I took a liking to named Robin. He was around my brother John's age and had a silver front tooth just like Johnny's. I now had all these neighbor kids as playmates.

I liked to steal Dad's Old Gold Cigarettes and walk around the trailer park, smoking. One time I was walking past Buzzy and Diane's house with a couple of kids from the trailer park. I noticed a big black garbage bag under the porch of the trailer in front of our house, and over to the right. My curiosity got the best of me and I dragged the trash bag out from under the porch. When I opened the bag, I found what looked like tightly-wound grass cuttings.

When Diane opened her door, she caught me snooping through the bag. "Oh, you're just in time!" she said, "Do you want a brownie?"

"Sure!" I said. I didn't realize what I was looking at in the bag. So, I had no idea that Diane's offer of the brownie was actually a ploy to distract me from the garbage bag full of marijuana.

Diane told me that she and Buzzy had found the bag floating in the ocean at Dunedin Beach by Honeymoon Island. Apparently, drug smugglers get as close to shore as possible. That way, they can jump out of the boat when the Coast Guard is after them. Since they got so close to shore, drugs often washed up on the beach. Whoever was around would find them. Buzzy and Diane sold some of the pot and distributed some of it to their friends.

When I took a bite of the brownie, I didn't like the taste of it at all. The next thing I knew, everything began to seem very funny.

Some local kids and I built a fort on the outskirts of the trailer park and that's where we went to smoke cigarettes and roll joints. My brother John had a Laredo cigarette-rolling machine. We would borrow it and take it with us to the fort, along with the pot.

I tried pot a few times but didn't really like it. I only smoked it now and then. But I got a contact high from being in the fort with the others who were smoking pot. That always gave me the giggles. I didn't like pot because when I smoked it, I couldn't stop laughing.

Buzzy sold a motorcycle to my parents. We had only owned it about a week when my brother John had an accident on it. He wiped out on the gravel and got all scraped up. Not only was he hurting, he was afraid to come home. He worried about what Dad would do to him when he found out. So, he went to a friend's house and called Mom instead.

Thankfully, John didn't get in any trouble. Mom and Dad both understood that the accident was exactly that—an accident. At times like this, you could feel that Dad loved us. He was just glad that John was alive.

Before the accident, John had been playing a lot of football. Afterwards, he started having trouble with his knee and wasn't able to play as much. He began lifting weights instead. To this day, he lifts weights for two hours each day.

Around this time, I met Eddie, a boy in the neighborhood. He was quiet, brooding and artistic. He drew me a picture in colored pencils and pastels. I loved it so much, I kept it until a couple of years ago.

His family lived in one of the nicest houses in a subdivision across from the trailer park where we lived. They even had a lake in their backyard. We trailer-park kids would jump the fence surrounding the subdivision where Eddie lived, and go swimming in the lake. I thought the lake was great—but the really amazing thing was the fact that he lived in a *house*, not a trailer. He had space between his family's house and the other houses.

I was about twelve at the time and Eddie was sixteen. At that age, four years was a huge age difference. I'm not sure how my parents would have felt about me spending time with a boy who was so much older. The truth was, they weren't around enough to even notice.

When Eddie and I were together, we usually stayed in the trailer park. One time, though, we went for a ride down a beautiful country road. I don't remember Eddie ever holding my hand or kissing me. He wasn't mushy like silver-toothed Johnny. But he was definitely my boyfriend—or rather, he told me I was his girlfriend.

The night he told me that I was his girlfriend, I thought, *Whatever.* Then I jumped into the lake to go swimming. Since my parents were away so much, we kids were left up to our own devices. That's how I ended up doing a lot of night swimming.

The horse track was one of the places my parents loved to go when they were off doing their own thing. Mom liked to gamble and Dad liked to play pool. So, it wasn't unusual for them to start the evening at the Horseshoe Bar and then head to the track.

With Dad playing pool and Mom betting on the horses, neither of them was holding down a job. We were living off the various checks Dad was collecting. Between the drinking and the late nights, it wasn't surprising when my parents started fighting again.

One night around this time, Dad found my diary, and started walking around the house, reading passages from it aloud. Mom was cooking dinner at the time. She didn't pay too much attention to what was happening.

When Dad got to the part about my boyfriend, skinny dipping, and other things I knew he wouldn't approve of, I panicked. I never went skinny-dipping myself. The other kids did it when it was dark outside but I would have rather died than take off my suit. But I knew that Dad would never believe me. He already called me a whore sometimes, just for spending time with guy friends.

"Give me back my diary!" I yelled, chasing him around our trailer.

He just laughed louder.

I jumped up, trying to grab it out of his hands.

He held my diary even higher and kept laughing and mocking me.

So, I hauled off and punched him in the stomach as hard as I could. His stomach was so hard, I hurt my hand when I hit him.

He buckled over, but he didn't bend low enough for me to grab my diary away from him.

I turned and ran as fast as I could, out the door, and down the street. It was getting dark outside by then. I found a neighbor who was willing to let me hide out there until the coast was clear. I stayed away until I thought everyone would be asleep in my house and then snuck back in.

Sure enough, everyone was fast asleep. The next morning, it was as if the whole incident had never happened. My dad didn't mention the diary or me hitting him and neither did my mom.

I never asked for my diary back and have no idea what became of it. But that was the last diary I ever kept. I had always kept one up until then but that incident with my dad cured me of the habit. I had learned my lesson.

I knew it was foolish to believe I had gotten away with punching my dad in the stomach. A short time after that, I was standing at the sink, doing dishes. (I had always been the resident dishwasher.) I was hurrying to get them done so I could go outside and run around. I was raring to get out the door. I was already dressed in my runnin' around clothes—my light-colored hip-huggers with patches I had sewn on with my own hands. They were my favorite pants of all time.

Dad had told me time and time again that these pants looked ratty. Of course, he was right but that was the point. They had holes in them, and were softly frayed in just the right way. On that day, he came up behind me while I was doing the dishes, and ripped them right off of me. He left me standing there in my underpants.

"You are not wearing these pants out of the house ever again!" he said.

I was mortified and furious. I ran into my room and locked the door. I refused to come out. I wanted so badly to ask my mom to sew my pants back together. But I knew she couldn't fight with my dad over my pants. I knew I had to pick my battles. So that day, I lost my favorite pair of pants.

About a week later, as I came in the house after playing, Dad started yelling at me. "You didn't do your chores! Look at this sink. There's dishes in it!"

All it took was one dish in the sink, and I was going down. That was my dad. He was such a fanatic, with his finger-tests for dust. I was becoming a teenager by then and was really getting sick of his iron fist. All I wanted to do was go out and play with my friends like a normal kid.

I was starting to get an adolescent mouth on me, too. So, I said, "Why can't somebody else do the dishes?" I said.

My brothers already had their own assigned chores. They did boy things like taking out the garbage and helping my dad in the yard.

When I mouthed off to my dad, he hit me upside the back of my head. I was standing in the kitchen at the time. I spun around and hit my head on the cupboard above me, which held drinking glasses. Then I was out cold on the floor.

When I came to, I lay there for a few minutes. I was hoping that maybe if I waited long enough, Dad would go away.

I could hear my mother screaming, "You need to quit it! You're gonna kill her!"

"She's alright," said Dad. "Get her up."

Then I got sent to my room and grounded. When I was very young, I sometimes went to bed bawling after Dad scolded or beat me. Mom and Dad left me there to cry. No one came in to rub my back and comfort me. No one came in to tell me it was all going to be okay. I always thought it was cold of them to just leave me there to cry myself to sleep.

But now, when Dad hit me really hard and sent me to my room, he usually started to feel badly about it after an hour or so. He would tell me to come out of my room. Then he'd say, "I didn't mean to hit you so hard but you need to listen to me and do what you're told!"

Sometimes after Dad disciplined me and got to feeling badly about it, he would let me sit on his lap. Then he'd put his arm around me in a rare show of affection. He'd lick his lips and give me a big, slobbery kiss like a doggie. If it was nighttime, he would tell me to give him and Mom a kiss goodnight. If I wasn't too mad about being hit, I would go ahead and kiss them goodnight.

It was rare for my dad to touch me in any affectionate way. I got the feeling he went out of his way *not* to touch me. Maybe he worried that he would give the impression that he was doing something wrong. I also figured that growing up in an orphanage, he never got the loving touch and didn't know how to give it.

As I got older, Dad had to try harder to maintain his control over me. So, our fights became more intense. I was challenging his authority and he didn't like that. He expected me to know my place, shut up, and obey.

He would say to me, "Suzette Renee, who the hell do you think you are, talking back to me?"

"I'm Suzette Renee! That's who I am."

I had things to say but my dad wasn't having it. I wanted to tell him that hurting me in the name of loving me was wrong.

At least Grandma Margaret gushed over me. Whenever she called our house to talk to Mom, I would start bawling. I loved her so much and I wanted to talk to her and feel her loving me. I would cry into the phone, and she would talk and somehow make everything all better.

When I was little and Mom was at work, Grandma Margaret was the one who always had time for me. She was very religious and often read the Bible to me. My own mother never went to church unless someone was getting baptized or something. But Grandma had been raised in a convent and kept up her religious ways. I was glad she had passed them down to me, even if they had skipped a generation and missed my mom.

Even though I knew Grandma liked my brothers more than me, I still felt her love for me. She just liked boys more in general.

This was a time of life when our family was really unstable, so we didn't see Grandma Margaret much. It seemed like she would wait until we got more stable and then come back around.

THIRTEEN

Y FRIENDS AND I walked around the trailer park, smoking cigarettes. Sometimes we went into the woods to the fort we had built. We would pick up each of the neighbor kids along the way. If we got to one of the neighbor kids' houses and they weren't quite finished with their chores, we would go into their house and wait.

I really liked the parents of my friend Robin with the silver front tooth. Everyone in the family was really tall. Or, maybe it just seemed that way to me because I was always real petite and skinny. Robin's dad called me Lil' Bit. I thought that was endearing.

One time, I was waiting in their house for Robin to finish his chores and the parents were watching *Hee Haw* on T.V.

They asked me, "Do you want to stay for dinner?"

I looked at them all sitting there. It was obvious to me that they were already squished in around the table. There was no room for me.

I said, "But where would I sit?"

They had already pushed two tables together to make one big one. Their chairs were already so close, they were touching. But somehow, they found room for me. Once everyone scooted over to make room for me, they handed me a big plate of spaghetti noodles, with meat sauce and garlic bread. The sauce covered the whole plate.

The dad in that family seemed to be a big foodie and the mom seemed like his slave. He would sit in his recliner and yell, "Bring the food in!"

They seemed like Edith and Archie Bunker, and that reminded me of the way my dad sometimes treated my mom.

Any time we were walking around the trailer park and Buzzy and

Diane saw us, they would invite us over to party. So, in the evenings when Mom and Dad were down at the bar playing pool, I'd be at Buzzy and Diane's. They were about five years younger than my parents and always seemed to have alcohol and marijuana at their parties.

When I was in the sixth or seventh grade in junior high school in Palm Harbor, a race war started between the blacks and the whites. I was raised around both races, so I was never in the middle of any of that. Even though it wasn't my fight, it was hard to avoid the conflict happening all around me.

One day, I was in the hallway at school, getting something out of my locker. I was standing there for the longest time, trying to remember the combination to my lock. I finally remembered it, got the lock off my locker, and reached inside to get a book or something.

Right at that moment, someone in a fighting mood came by and shoved my head right into my open locker. It was a classmate from my next class, a black girl.

She pushed me so hard, my head bounced backwards and I fell. As far as I was concerned, assaulting someone from behind when they can't defend themselves is fighting dirty. I was really upset over it.

In my next class, I could see this girl sitting in front of me, off to the right, near the front door. Instead of telling someone what this girl had done to me, or talking to her about it, I sat in the classroom stewing over it.

I was asking myself, *What am I going to do? Take her shit? Or do something about it?*

I got myself so worked up during class, staring at her from behind, I didn't have it in me to let it go. So, when the bell rang at the end of class and everyone poured out into the hallway, I went after her.

I was ready to assert some independence and stand up for myself. The only way I knew to do that was through violence. Those were the coping tools I'd picked up at home, from my dad and my brother John. I tore the girl up. I knocked her off her platform shoes, and started pounding her face into the floor.

As I was punching her, I was saying, "I'm not taking your shit!"

I was releasing all the anger I had toward everyone. All the crap I'd had to take at home from my dad and my brother had built up inside me. I was starting to feel really angry at everyone for everything.

Unfortunately, we got into it right by the principal's office. The principal pulled me off of the girl and took me into his office.

"What about her?" I demanded to know. "Why doesn't she have to come in?"

"Because *you* were the aggressor."

By failing to tell anyone about what this girl had done to me, I had set myself up. It now looked like I had gone after her for no reason, totally unprovoked.

I was suspended from school, and told that the principal would be calling my parents personally to tell them about my suspension.

I was really scared of what my dad would do to me when he found out. I had one thing going for me—the fact that this suspension took place on a Friday. I knew that on Friday nights, my parents went to the bar. Sometimes they left the house around the same time I got out of school. Sometimes they had dinner with us kids and then headed to the bar. Dad would shoot pool and Mom would sit at the bar, nursing a drink. They pretty much always stayed until the bar closed around midnight or 1:00 in the morning.

I felt guilty for getting into a fight and getting myself suspended. I was entering a time in my life where I felt guilty for a lot of things, many of which weren't my fault. Not only did I feel guilty about the fight and about getting suspended, I was also worried. I kept wondering what the girl's people might do to me whenever I did go back to school. I had a feeling they would beat me up pretty badly. I figured that, even if I rode the bus and had the protection of the bus driver, they would find me in between classes.

The Friday night I got suspended, I partied with a bunch of friends at Buzzy and Diane's mobile home. As the hours went by, we got really, really drunk. We were singing our heads off, and having a great time.

When the party ended, I made my way home and got into bed. I passed out before my parents got home, so no one was the wiser.

I went to sleep happy that night. My parents didn't yet know about my suspension. And I had friends who had my back—something I didn't get at home. For most of my early life, I felt like I was closer to my friends than I was to my family. I really started to value, appreciate and enjoy my friendships.

The next night, Saturday, I was walking around the trailer park, collecting my friends as I went. I picked up my close friend Teresa and another close girlfriend. Once again, we ended up at Buzzy and Diane's. When we arrived, they were drinking and smoking pot.

Ed was there—a tall guy who was older and considered himself my boyfriend. He was protective over me, and that felt good, considering that protection was in short supply at home. I took a shine to him because of his protectiveness toward me. I don't remember kissing him or holding his hand.

Everyone was laughing and having fun. Suddenly, Buzzy said to me, "Come on over here and sit by me."

Ed gave me a funny look.

"Well, he told me to sit by him!" I said, by way of explanation. I didn't think twice about it.

"You know what would be a good idea?" said Buzzy. "If you went to your house and got us some of your dad's pain pills!"

Wow! How cool! I said to myself. *He's counting on me to bring the party supplies.* Being trusted by the adults made me feel really included and important.

Buzzy patted me on the back and steered me toward the door of their mobile home. Drunk, I stumbled outside and headed to my family's trailer.

Nobody was home when I got there, so I went into the medicine cabinet. There were so many pills, and my vision was so blurry, I couldn't decide which ones to take. I dumped an assortment into a pill bottle and went back over to Buzzy and Diane's house.

When I got back to the party, I handed the pills over to Buzzy. He seemed to know which pills were which, and started handing them out. We all sang songs and hung out for a while longer.

One by one, everyone at the party started to slowly fall asleep. They would be talking, lay their head down for a minute, and be out like a light. Even Diane was asleep in the back bedroom.

"Wow! We must have been partying for a while," said Buzzy. "Everyone's fallen asleep! Let's you and me have another drink."

We had another drink and then he said, "Would you like to go for a ride in my car? I know you like to go fast."

Buzzy had a souped-up Chevy with big tires and a loud muffler. It was a real muscle car. I remembered how exciting it was when he took me for a ride on his motorcycle once.

I said, "Oh, my God! I would love to go for a ride in your car!"

I was only twelve years old at the time. I thought that having this older guy invite me for a ride in his car was cool.

We were in Buzzy's car and he was driving us down the road. It was fun and loud, and I was hanging my head out the window so the wind could blow through my hair. I was high and going for this great ride.

When Buzzy got on the highway, I didn't really give it a thought. I'd been on the highway with him before. I am a car sleeper under any circumstances and that night, I was drunk and dozed off.

When I opened my eyes again, I didn't recognize the landscape. I said, "Where are we going? It seems like we've been driving for a long time!"

He told me that we were headed to a town with the word holiday in the name. It was about twenty miles from Palm Harbor. When we got there, he pulled over. He had a big jug of whiskey with him and took a swig. Then he passed it to me.

I was thirsty so I took a drink. It burned going down, so I handed it back to him. I told him that I didn't want any more of it. It was taking everything in me to stay awake. I was so drunk and tired, I was numb.

Buzzy pulled the car off the highway and into a secluded area. "I'm just going to turn around here," he said. Then he kept driving, deeper and deeper into the woods.

I thought, *We can do a three-point turn anywhere. Why is he still driving?*

By the time I could have gotten the question out of my mouth, Buzzy finally stopped. "I'm going to get out and go to the bathroom," he said.

I waited in the car. I was looking around at our surroundings and realized that there was nobody anywhere. I had absolutely no idea where we were. And since I'd dozed off in the car, I had no idea what road we had taken to get there.

Buzzy seemed to be perfectly straight. He had made everyone else pass out but made sure he could still drive and function. That's when I knew something was wrong. He got back in the car and started moving toward me to kiss me.

I didn't have those feelings for him and didn't want to kiss him. But it seemed harmless enough. I thought to myself, *Alright, I guess.*

So, I kissed him. Then I said, "Okay, can we stop now?"

Instead of stopping, Buzzy jumped into the back seat and tried to pull me with him.

I was starting to feel sick. "I'm not feeling well," I said.

"Just come back here for a minute. You'll feel better and then I'll get you home."

Buzzy started mauling me and pulling off my clothes.

I was trying to push him away and pull my clothes back on but my body felt like jelly. *I think my best bet is to just relax,* I thought. *Maybe if I relax, he'll do whatever he's doing and then stop and leave me alone.*

Buzzy had his clothes off by now. He finally got my pants and underwear off. He was trying to penetrate me. At that point, the fighter in me woke back up. I started squeezing my legs together and trying to roll over. I was so upset, I started crying.

I asked myself, *Oh, my God! What's going on?*

He grabbed my hand and put it on his penis. It wasn't that I was afraid of him, exactly. I trusted him for the most part. But I didn't like where this was all heading.

I was crying and saying no over and over again. I was trying to keep my legs squeezed together and doing my best to roll over. I was fighting so hard, I was managing to keep him from getting inside me.

He had really long hair and was sweating by now, so his hair was getting all tangled up and falling in my face.

I was blubbering and spit-crying. My mother had never talked to me about sex. So, I didn't really know what getting inside of me meant. I felt like he liked me and just wanted to be close to me—but he was being a brute. He was hurting me by trying to get inside me.

I just wanted to go home. I was trying to look out the back window of the car. I was hoping to spot either a place to run to or someone who could help me. I didn't scream because I didn't see anyone around.

I must have said to myself a hundred times in my mind, *There's no one around to help me so I'm going to have to help myself! It's up to me . . . it's up to me . . . it's up to me.*

FOURTEEN

BUZZY SUDDENLY SEEMED to realize that he was not going to get anywhere with me. So, he put his clothes back on and told me to put mine back on. He jumped back into the front seat and I did too. He took another swig from the whiskey bottle and then handed it to me so I could take a drink.

I'm sure he was frustrated but he never got mad at me. He just drove us back to town.

I felt really beat up as we drove home. I was also horrified to realize we had been gone for so long that it was now dusk. I started to panic, realizing I was going to be in serious trouble for getting home after dark. I was anxious to get home as fast as we could. I couldn't believe it when Buzzy drove right past the trailer park where we lived.

"Where are you going?" I asked, panicked.

"To get cigarettes."

I was thinking, *Oh, no! That's a few miles away!* I was so upset.

We finally pulled into the parking lot of the convenience store. Buzzy left the car running and got out. As he headed inside to get his cigarettes, another car pulled up behind us, its brakes squealing.

Buzzy's wife, Diane, jumped out of the car. She was furious when she saw me sitting in Buzzy's car. I knew I must have looked like a sight, coming down from this drunken party. But she was at the same party—up until the driving part with Buzzy, anyway. So, she shouldn't have been too surprised by my appearance. Of course, I had also been mauled by Buzzy after the party. So, I looked like a mess.

Diane started banging on the car window, trying to get me to open the door. Thankfully, the car doors were locked. She yelled through the window, threatening to tell my dad. Everyone in the neighborhood knew that my dad beat me. She knew if she told him, I would get a beating.

I stayed put. I said to myself, *There's no way I'm getting out of this car!*

She kept screaming at me through the window, saying, "I'm gonna tell your dad!"

I was scared. Diane was older than me and bigger than me. I knew that my only hope was to stay in the car. She could have laid me out flat if I got out. I got so scared, I started shaking. I was relieved when Buzzy came out of the store.

When Diane saw him, she started screaming all sorts of things at him. She demanded to know where the hell we had been and what the hell we'd been doing. Buzzy ignored her and got back in the car.

Diane went back to her car, got inside, and spun off. Then Buzzy silently drove us back to his place. He got out of the car without saying a single word to me and went inside his trailer to face the music.

I jumped out of the car and ran towards home. As I ran, I could hear Diane screaming at Buzzy. I was shaking like a leaf, and terrified of what Diane might tell my dad.

When I got home, there was nobody there. It was a miracle. I got into the shower so I could wash Buzzy's sweat off of me. All I wanted was to feel better.

When I got out of the shower, I put on a soft, silky, pretty green nighty. I was thinking to myself, *Dad's gonna kill me!*

I knew that, come Monday, I was going to have to face the music over being suspended. The school hadn't been able to reach Mom and Dad on Friday to tell them I'd been suspended for fighting. Come Monday, the truth would come out. Dad was then going to have *three* real good reasons for doing me in: the suspension, the alcohol-and-drug party at Buzzy and Diane's, and me being in the car with Buzzy afterward.

I was terrified. I figured I might as well get the killing over with before Dad could get a hold of me. I went into Dad's medicine cabinet. I opened up every bottle of pills I could find and started swallowing them. I took them and took them until I couldn't swallow any more.

John came home and found me passed out on the couch. He started yelling at me, "Get up and get the dishes done! Dad's coming home pretty soon."

He shook me and shook me but I wouldn't wake up. Then he dragged me off the couch and into the bathroom. I still didn't wake up. He ran the water in the sink and splashed it on my face. By that point, he realized there was something wrong with me. I was still passed out.

He called our parents at the Horseshoe Bar where they hung out. When he got them on the phone, he told them, "Something's wrong with Suzette! I can't get her to wake up."

Mom and Dad rushed home.

While the paramedics were taking me to the hospital, my heart stopped more than once. They had to keep reviving me. I spent thirty-two hours in a coma. When I woke up from the coma, I was hooked up to machines. I could see my mom standing above me and my dad standing off to the side by himself.

I was half conscious, looking down at myself, trying to make sense of everything I was seeing. My mom later told me that these were my first words as I started to regain consciousness: "The butler did it."

As my head started to clear, I remembered what had happened. I thought, *Oh, my God! I'm still here? I don't want to be alive anymore. I'm going to be in so much trouble with Dad!*

But when I looked at my parents, they didn't seem mad. Then I was waking up in a different room—not the one where I was hooked up to machines. This room was sterile and blindingly white. The bed was the only thing in the room other than the bathroom.

People kept coming in and out of my room. And, any time I tried to sit up, I threw up the black charcoal they used to pump my stomach. And when I wasn't throwing up, I was running into the bathroom.

I spent a few days in that all-white room. I was puking, running to the bathroom, and feeling like I had the all-time worst case of the flu. Little by little, I started to feel better.

While I was in the hospital, I wondered about Daddy John telling Mom that her side of the family was eccentric and crazy. I didn't *feel* crazy. I was just doing my best to survive my crazy home life—and my abusive dad.

Mom felt like her side of the family was eccentric—not crazy—and filled with colorful, independent people. They sure seemed colorful to me. My mother's grandfather, for one, was a boxer into his eighties. Mom's father's sister, Aunt Ethel, was known as the queen of the gays. (She was the one whose hair Mom bleached to the point where it fell out.)

In the 1970s, the gays were coming out of the closet and many were being rejected by their families. Great-Aunt Ethel made a community and a family for them. Many of the gays felt like throwaway people before she came along and made them feel welcome. She was forever single and in her older years, the gays *she* looked after looked after *her*, both financially and emotionally.

As the story goes, Aunt Ethel had done some performing in the gay-bar district in Detroit in the Sixties and Seventies. That was where a lot of the gays lived and performed back in those days, doing transvestite shows. She never had a family, but I didn't get the impression that she was a lesbian either.

She had apparently been sexually assaulted by her stepfather and got pregnant. When she gave birth, her mother (Grandma Tuttle) took the baby. When Aunt Ethel woke up after sleeping off the exhaustion of labor, she asked Grandma, "Where's my baby?"

Grandma simply said, "The baby's gone."

No one knew whether Grandma took the baby out on the day of its birth and buried it in the snow or gave it to somebody. In any event, it was tragic and traumatic for Aunt Ethel to be assaulted and then give birth and have the baby taken from her. This trauma may have led to her devotion to the gay community and her empathy for those who felt like outcasts. I loved knowing that my great-aunt found comfort and solace with the gays.

Then there was the violin teacher who was my mother's aunt. I think of her as Aunt Mable but Mable may or may not have been her actual name. When Mom was a little girl, Aunt Mable lived down the street with her husband and mother. When she played, the sound was exquisite. This strong, independent violinist earned her living by teaching the violin. She recorded many forty-five-RPM records we listened to on an old wind-up record player.

In that era, independence was not a quality that was necessarily admired in women. Aunt Mable's husband was jealous of the attention she got from her social circle and her violin students. He felt that his wife's place was in the home. One day, he snapped and bludgeoned her about the head with a hammer, and then he took an axe and also killed her mother.

Then there was my mother's father, Grandpa Larry. During the Great Depression, he was a well-paid engineer with a good job. When he lost his job, he became a bootlegger in order to support his family. Grandpa eventually turned to the bottle and worked the rides at Cedar Point Amusement Park. He stayed in that job for more than thirty years.

During his days as a bootlegger, Grandpa Larry worked for Al Capone's crew. He ran liquor into dry states like Michigan and Ohio. Whenever I asked Grandpa to tell me about Al Capone, he turned away from me and refused to say anything.

The only time I ever remember Grandpa telling me anything about Al Capone was when I asked, "Grandpa? Did he have cool hair?"

"Yes, he did . . . but most of the time, his hair was hidden under a hat."

My maternal grandmother was married to a man before Grandpa Larry and may not have been legally divorced from him. This would explain why she never married Grandpa Larry. It would also explain why Mom and Aunt Peggy always said that Grandma had "one and a half husbands."

Whenever I heard stories of my mother's family, I thought they sounded very colorful and beautiful. They were definitely a product of the times and circumstances. They each made the best of life, remained true to themselves, and never cared about society's cookie-cutter expectations of how they should live their lives.

My mother herself was a quiet, proper, graceful lady. She wasn't eccentric like the rest of her family. She was plain but beautiful and wore her dark hair in a 1950s Doris Day coif. When the 1970s rolled around, she piled her hair on top of her head in a beehive hairdo and wear go-go boots.

Nobody asked me anything about what had put me in the hospital. Everyone acted as if nothing had happened. That was a little bit strange—but I was grateful. I was already embarrassed, and felt like I had done something wrong . . . done *plenty* wrong! I was horrified over everything that had happened.

I had been drinking. I had been taking drugs. I had let someone's husband take me for a drive, alone. I had put myself in a position where a man was trying to get me out of my clothes and put his thing inside me. Then, to top it all off, I was so scared of the punishment I'd get from Dad, I had taken a handful of drugs and overdosed.

The list of things I had done wrong was huge. Maybe that's why no one said a word to me about it. Maybe they didn't know where to start.

Once I got to feeling a bit better, I was moved out of the all-white room and into a regular hospital room. I have a vague memory of my mom coming to see me a couple of times while I was still in the all-white room. I would later find out that I had been in the psychiatric ward of Mease Hospital, and they allowed only minimal family interaction for about thirty days.

I liked Mrs. Woods, one of my nurses, and Bryce, an orderly. They were both very nice to me and I think of them often.

Mom brought me art supplies when she visited. She knew I liked to sketch, color, do needlepoint, and paint by numbers. That was wonderful—but nothing was as wonderful as the fact that no one was asking me to tell them what had happened.

I continued to heal. During the latter part of the month I was in the hospital, I started to feel a bit feisty. So, I went into the day room where everyone gathered to play cards. I liked to bend the cards at the corner so they made a popping sound.

One of the other patients I was playing cards with would say, "Oh, my

God, you've got to stop doing that! It's driving me crazy!" It reminded me of how aggravated my brother John would get with me.

While I was there, we also had group therapy. At first, I didn't want to speak in the group. The lady who was running the group wanted to get everybody to interact. But since I was only twelve years old at the time, I was treated a bit differently. They didn't insist that I talk. So, I just sat there and listened.

I never did end up joining in because I was too uncomfortable, but I listened. I learned a big life lesson from listening to everyone else: people of all ages, rich and poor, have problems. It wasn't just me. I realized that I would have trouble from time to time in my life. I was going to have to figure out a way to handle it. I couldn't keep trying to use suicide as a solution.

Towards the end of my stay there, I did open up to Mrs. Woods and Bryce a little bit. We were all night owls. But I never said anything specific and neither of them ever dug for details.

By then, I was feeling better and stronger. I was starting to wish that somebody *would* ask me about it. Now, I did want to talk about it but I didn't want to be the first one to bring it up.

I would think to myself, *There's that nice-looking Bryce. I could talk to him about it, if only he would bring up the subject.*

Bryce had told me that he was in his early twenties and had two brothers. I had always felt like one of the boys, myself. So, I knew that Bryce would have been easy to talk to. It seemed like I was always on the verge of talking to him but I couldn't work up my nerve.

Even though Mrs. Woods and I didn't talk about what had happened, we did have long talks. I told her my problems with my dad. She gave me some pointers on things I could do that might help when he was being hard on me.

Later, after I left the hospital, I would end up going back to visit Mrs. Woods. I showed up at the hospital front desk and said, "I'd like to go back and speak with Mrs. Woods in the psychiatric ward." I acted like I lived there.

During my follow-up treatment at the hospital, I was under the care of Dr. Black. He told my mom that she needed to get away from my dad because he was bad for me. Dr. Black explained that my dad's actions would negatively affect me in the long-term. That was the first and only time anyone ever spoke up for me and pointed out the obvious danger posed by my dad.

I would often think to myself, *Aren't people seeing the way Dad treats us? People must know! They must be afraid of Dad. Me too. He's scary! He's got guns and knives. And when he gets mad, he's always threatening to blow people up in their cars or while they are sleeping!*

While I was hospitalized, my boyfriend Ed came to see me. He came to the window, which actually opened. (These days, I think they keep all the hospital windows tightly sealed.) I could see my parents off in the distance, standing by their car.

"How are you doing, Suzette?" said Ed. "I wanted to come by and tell you I love you. And I want you to have this."

I reached out my hand and accepted the little box he handed me. Then I turned around and walked away. I wanted to look at whatever it was privately, and not be under pressure to react in the moment. Inside was a little diamond ring, and it was very pretty.

This gift from Ed made me feel really good, especially considering what I had found out: my friends had ratted me out when news of my overdose got out. I found this out as soon as I woke up from the coma. Mom said, "Don't worry. Everybody told us about everything you've been doing for a long time, and it's okay . . ."

Mom named names and told me that she knew about me partying and smoking pot. She also knew everything else I'd been doing wrong. "It's all out in the open now, Suzette. We know what's been going on."

I felt really betrayed by my friends. I thought to myself, *I guess my friends are not really my friends after all. They didn't protect me.*

At the same time, I understood why my friends had ratted me out. None of them knew whether or not I was going to make it. I had technically died and the paramedics revived me. So, they figured they had better spill the beans and tell my family everything I had ever done wrong. They wanted my family to have the full picture.

I had always tried to protect my parents from the bad things I did. Now they knew everything. I knew that my dad usually thought the worst of me anyway, but I hated to think that my mom thought badly of me.

I was torn. I understood why my friends ratted me out but that didn't make me feel any less betrayed. So, when Ed came to see me and gave me the ring, it was healing for me. He was a quiet guy and never spoke much. He simply cared about me, and that made me feel good.

FIFTEEN

AFTER THIRTY-TWO DAYS in the hospital, I was released. I had been out on a day pass or two but going home was different. On the one hand, I felt ready to get back into normal daily life. At the same time, everything felt strange. As I returned home, I knew I had matured.

My parents moved us into a house on Highland Avenue in Dunedin. Highland Avenue sat on the border between Dunedin and Clearwater and went all the way through town. It was the first Florida house we bought.

When I looked around the neighborhood, I saw all these houses that had been painted red, white and blue for the 1976 Bicentennial. I had only been hospitalized for a month but it felt like I was coming out into a whole new world.

About a month after I got out of the hospital, my mom drove me to the courthouse. She didn't tell me why she was taking me there. That was a good move on her part. If I had known beforehand, I definitely would have started freaking out.

When we got inside a conference room at the courthouse, I asked her, "What are we doing here?"

"They just want to ask you some questions, Suzette. Tell them the truth. And then we can leave."

In the conference room was a lady with her stenography machine. An attorney asked me questions, and the stenographer typed away.

They were taking my deposition, so that I could tell them what Buzzy had done to me. Instead, I told them nothing—not that Buzzy had given me alcohol, not that I had gone home and gotten the pills out of my dad's stash in the medicine cabinet, and not what Buzzy had done to me in the car.

I wasn't keeping quiet as a way to protect him. I was just too embarrassed to say anything. I could never have said the words penis, vagina, or even sex—not with my mom sitting right by my side. Even today I have trouble saying those words. If Mom hadn't been there, it might have been a different story.

Even though I didn't say a word about Buzzy during my deposition, the authorities were able to move forward with prosecuting him. I found out years later that Buzzy was sent to prison for three years for giving alcohol to me because I was a minor. Apparently, he was already either on parole or probation at the time of the incident, making the offense a parole or probation violation.

I'm not sure whether or not Buzzy also got in trouble for putting me in his car and driving me out of town. The one thing he definitely did not get in trouble for, and should have, was sexually assaulting me. But no one ever knew because I never told. Buzzy and I were the only two people who knew, and Diane suspected something. I never did find out whether she had also gotten into trouble. After all, the party had started at their house.

It was strange to find out that Buzzy had gone to prison. I never did find out exactly how the prosecuting attorney had gotten enough evidence to convict. I figured it was probably a combination of things. I was a twelve-year-old girl who was given alcohol and drugs that were still in my system when I was admitted to the hospital. And there were plenty of witnesses from the party—all my so-called friends who had ratted me out.

I enrolled at Dunedin Junior High, relieved not to have to return to the school where I'd had the fight with the girl. I was still worried about her and her friends coming after me, seeking revenge. At Dunedin Junior High, race was not an issue. The student body was made up of about

80% whites and 20% blacks and everyone seemed to coexist without any trouble.

Even though I wasn't quite thirteen years old, I was starting to feel like a young lady. I spent more time styling my hair. I was also starting to take more notice of boys.

Meanwhile, across the street, my friend Debbie was teaching me what it meant to be a southern lady. Debbie's mom and dad, Derwood and Etheline, owned a chain of movie theaters. They were from Georgia and they were real southern people, with the accents and all. I thought they were so awesome.

Whenever I went to Debbie's house, it seemed like her mom was busy cooking. The food she cooked was nothing I'd ever seen before. I would think to myself, *My lord! Look at all this southern food!*

Debbie's mom cooked red gravy, sautéing big chunks of tomatoes in flour and then serving it over biscuits or grits. When I was invited over to their house for dinner, I would pitch in, cracking beans and shucking corn. It wasn't my first time shucking corn but I'd never shucked corn and cracked beans all in the same meal.

Debbie's mom was an Elvis Presley fanatic and had black velvet paintings of Elvis in the house. Every time I went to her house, Elvis was playing on the stereo.

Debbie's family's so cool, I said to myself. *All we ever hear at my house is country!* My family liked traditional old-school country artists like Hank Williams and Johnny Cash.

Debbie's dad worked a lot and when he was home, he was often in his room. He didn't seem to be very good with people, especially when compared to his wife. She was real friendly and a good businesswoman. She handled the hiring, firing and accounting end of things.

That was my first exposure to a woman handling those tasks. I saw the value and importance in what she did, and she became an early role model for me. I used what I learned from her when I later had my own hair-styling business.

Debbie and I both had different last names than the rest of our families, and we both smoked cigarettes. We also seemed to get interested in the same things, like CB radios. My CB handle was Sunshine. Hers was Boogie Baby. We would talk to boys on the CB, and once we really got the hang of it, we started talking to truckers in their lingo.

Debbie and I went everywhere and did everything together. We became like sisters and we fought like sisters. We were both born in 1963, and we went to the same school but were not in the same classes.

We walked three miles to school together. Then, after school and on the weekends, we watched movies at the movie theaters owned by her parents. It was great having a friend whose parents owned movie theaters. We would get free popcorn, and sit and watch a movie over and over again.

We saw a lot of movies there, but the three that stand out in my memory are *The Exorcist, JAWS* and *Smoky and the Bandit.* Eventually, Debbie ended up working the concession stand at the theater. When we were old enough to date, we would bring our little boyfriends to the movie theater.

As I started to feel more like a young lady, and got interested in hair and makeup, I started thinking about being an extra in movies. I often noticed film shoots happening in our town. I thought maybe they would let me be in one of the movies. So, I would go to the set location. A couple of times I did get to be an extra, like the time I got to be in the stadium crowd in the baseball movie, *Long Gone.*

When Debbie and I weren't at school or the movies, we were usually at her house. But if we weren't at her house, she was at mine. She had two older brothers, one who was five or six years older than Debbie and me, and one around John's age. They were both gorgeous but neither one paid me any mind. They would say hi in passing but that was about it. I'm sure in their minds, I was nothing more than their little sister's friend.

I loved to look at these boys, and I followed them around whenever I could get away with it. The family had a garage apartment especially for the boys, with posters of some our favorite bands—Kiss, Pink Floyd and Wild Cherry, the band that sang *Play That Funky Music, White Boy.*

Between her great-looking brothers and all the delicious southern food, I loved being at Debbie's house. We liked to play our favorite songs over and over again and make up our own dances. She often got frustrated with me because I could never remember the steps she choreographed for us. My inability to remember things had everything to do with the head injury I sustained when I was young.

Sometimes we would go walking through our neighborhood after dark. We were always scared of running into this older kid who liked to run around without any shoes or shirt, scaring people. He was as big as an adult, baldheaded, and may or may not have still been a senior in high school. He was a wily guy. He liked hiding behind trees and then springing out when we least expected and scaring the daylights out of us.

There was something really off about this guy. I found out years later that all those times he was running around like a madman, he was actually trying to train himself for going into the Army. Sadly, he wasn't in the Army but a year when he got killed by friendly fire.

The local 7-11 convenience store was one of the hangouts for the neighborhood kids, so Debbie and I often went down there. There were gas pumps and a pinball machine inside. I met Cathy, one of my lifelong friends, at the pinball machine. We would steal Mad Dog 20/20 from behind the counter, and sneak out behind the convenience store to drink. Once we were done drinking it and smoking our cigarettes, we'd go back inside and play some more pinball.

Mad Dog wasn't the first thing I ever stole. When I was around nine years old, I was caught stealing nail polish and jewelry. Well, I wasn't *caught* so much as I was ratted out by my partner in crime—a little neighbor girl. Just my luck, she had an attack of conscience one day and spilled her guts.

When the girl's mom told my mom what I'd done, my mom was furious with me. Not only had I stolen things, I had lied about it for an entire month. Mom wasn't happy about me stealing but the fact that I'd lied really upset her.

I think she was genuinely disappointed in me. Up until then, she had believed everything I ever told her. When she found out what I'd done, she really blew her top and started chasing me around with a broom.

Dad never wanted to go anywhere other than the bar. His idea of eating dinner at a fancy restaurant was picking up food for take-out. He didn't enjoy family life and the stress of going places with us kids. He had never had family outings while he was growing up. He was most comfortable by himself in a room with the door closed, watching T.V. and yelling for everyone to be quiet.

So, I was surprised when Mom and Dad scored tickets to a Tampa Bay Buccaneers game. Dad actually seemed excited about going to this football game. On the day of the game, Mom and Dad started to walk out the door without me.

"Wait up!" I said.

"What do you mean?" they said. "You're not going!"

"What? Why not?"

"You have to stay home and watch Jake."

Dad had brought home our new dog, Jake, about a month beforehand. I loved Jake and thought he was an awesome dog. But I didn't want to stay home and dog-sit. Of course, my feelings didn't matter. I was out of luck. The boys got to go to the game, and I had to stay home alone with Jake.

About a month later, snow started falling in Florida! It was the first time I had ever seen it snow in Florida. I got so excited, all I wanted to do was run over to Debbie's to talk about the snow. So, I ran out the door, out of our backyard, and across the street to Debbie's. I totally forgot to shut the gate tightly.

I was hanging out with Debbie, listening to music and having fun. Hours went by. Finally, I realized I'd better get home, so I said goodbye to Debbie. When I got home, I realized I had accidentally let Jake out of the yard. Dad grounded me but at least I didn't get hit. (Jake returned to the house on his own.)

Another day, I was out running around when I should have been looking after Jake. When I got home, I saw that the dog had destroyed the house. He had chewed up the couch cushions, torn down the curtains, gnawed on the furniture, and shredded the phone cord. There was fluff from the couch cushions floating in the air. It looked like a bull had run through the house.

It was always a big deal for my parents any time we got new furniture. *I'm gonna die!* I said to myself. I'm not a big thinker but I take action, so I got busy. I started racing around, trying to quickly clean up the mess. But I only got about three minutes of cleaning done before my parents walked through the door.

They were seriously pissed off when they saw the mess. Dad got mad and started yelling at me. He said that I was now on restriction—additional restriction on top of the restriction I was already on. That was nothing new. It seemed like everything I did ended up with me on restriction.

SIXTEEN

I WAS GLAD THAT Dad had quit hitting me by then. Now, he punished me with restriction and verbal abuse. He was constantly calling me dumb or stupid.

I told myself, *Well, everyone has a different kind of smarts.*

I never found out why Dad stopped hitting me. Maybe he took pity on me after the overdose. Or, maybe Mom talked to him about it after the doctor at the hospital talked to *her* about it. As I mentioned, the doctor had told Mom that, for my safety, I needed to be away from Dad. Mom should have removed us kids from Dad after that talk with the doctor. But she couldn't bring herself to leave him.

Not long after the incidents related to me messing up on my Jake dog-sitting duties, I got in another kind of trouble. It all started when somebody gave me pot. I didn't smoke it very often but Debbie did. So, I was holding the joint for her. I hid it in a tampon holder.

Around that same time, Mom saw me stumble over something when I walked in the house. I wasn't smoking pot or taking drugs. I hadn't even had a beer. I was just clumsy that day. But Mom had found the joint I was holding for Debbie and jumped to the wrong conclusion.

Everyone had been watching me like a hawk since my overdose. When Mom found the joint, she panicked. She started shaking it, saying, "What is this, Suzette! Why do you have this? You are so in trouble!"

Mom and Dad made a call to the state and told them I was ungovernable. They saw signs of me heading down the wrong path and figured it was best to send me to a crisis home. I really believe my parents' hearts were in the right place. Between the boys, drugs, alcohol, and everything I had gone through in my life, they were genuinely trying to get me some help before I got older.

The crisis home was actually the residence of a family who had agreed to take me in. The parents already had four kids of their own, and they were housing a few other kids in crisis. So, there were about ten of us in the house, including the parents. Going to one of these homes was apparently the first step in the state system.

The family was really nice. While I was at their home, I came to enjoy following a routine. It gave me a sense of stability and security I had never felt before. Everybody got up in the morning, ate breakfast, and went to the same school. I got to feel for the first time what it was like to have structure.

The dad had once been in the military. I don't know whether he still had a military job or went to a civilian workplace. When he left for work, the mom stayed home with all the kids.

One day, I was downstairs watching *Charlie's Angels* on T.V. while the rest of the kids were upstairs. After a while, I went upstairs to see what everyone was doing. When I got upstairs, I found the kids all huddled together, huffing glue or getting high from an aerosol can. They had residue all over their faces. I thought they all looked really immature and stupid.

They put me in this place with all this going on when all I did wrong was hold a joint for a friend? I thought. *This is so unfair!*

One of the boys in the house really liked me. I thought he was cute, so right before I was supposed to leave to go home for a visit, I got into a make-out session with him. I ended up with hickeys all over my neck. I couldn't figure out how I was going to hide them. It was summertime, and too hot to be wrapping scarves around my neck.

It was just my luck that the one and only time my parents came and picked me up for a weekend visit turned out to be the very weekend I had hickeys on my neck. My parents decided I wasn't ready to come home, so that was the end of that. I think they were evaluating me all along to see whether or not I was ready to go home.

Any time throughout my life that I was going off the rails, Mom would tell me that I needed to straighten up my act. I blew it with my make-out session.

Dad said, "You need to learn to act like a lady! Your body is your temple. So, *treat it* like a temple! Stop letting people mess with you. Don't let anybody maul your body."

I couldn't wear short shorts, tank tops, or perfume. And when I started to color my hair blonde, Dad said it was whorish. He was the same way with Mom. I had heard him say similar things to her over the years about clothes she was wearing. But he was less harsh with her than he was with me.

After seeing hickeys on my neck at the crisis home, my parents were at a loss as to what to do with me. I got the impression that Mom felt like I was turning into a bad person, now that Dad couldn't beat me anymore. Or, maybe both of my parents felt that I wasn't doing everything I should have been doing to be a *good* person.

As far as I was concerned, I wasn't bad. The way I saw it, bad things happen to good people.

Mom and Dad called the social worker who was in charge of my case, and she found a group-home placement for me.

The group home was a nice big house in St. Petersburg. There were about ten kids living there. When I first got to the group home, I was very unhappy. I didn't appreciate the fact that my parents had left me in placement. I felt abandoned. But, since I had to stay there until I was released, I had to find a way to get through it.

The house mother was named Pam and she was married to Mike. Late at night, Mike would hole up in their bedroom and smoke pot. I'm sure he thought no one noticed. I may have been the only one who knew what he was doing. To me, it wasn't a big deal.

The days were structured, and that was fine with me. I enjoyed the routine of the place, just as I had in the crisis home. We had various activities and also spent time in a private one-room schoolhouse run by the state. In the after-school group sessions, I got to practice some of the lessons in expressing myself I'd learned in the hospital.

I would share feelings like, "It's not fair that I'm here. I don't belong here!" Later in life, in a transportation job where I was transporting inmates, I would hear the inmates say that and relate to how they were feeling.

Mom came to see me twice while I was there. When she visited me, she was wearing a beautiful dress and high boots, like a model. On one of Mom's two visits to me while I was in the group home, she came to my school. She was there to tell me that she was going to Minnesota with Dad. He needed another surgery.

A couple of days later, Grandma Lottie came from Ohio to see me at the group home. Grandma was from Poland and was very European in her ways. She had extremely long gray hair. She wore it in a braid that ran from one ear to the other, across the top of her head like a tiara. And, you could hardly understand her broken English.

She took me out to dinner. It was wonderful to be with her. It was the first time she had ever come to see me. Mom kept in touch with her through letters and photographs.

My parents were off to Minnesota and I was on my own at the group home. When we had Parents' Night at the home, my parents didn't come. I was hurt that they weren't there, even though I knew they were in Minnesota for Dad's surgery.

Mom sent me plenty of money so the lady in charge of the group home could buy me whatever I needed. It seemed like I had more than anyone else. I had never felt like we had so much until I was surrounded by kids who had so little.

Mom wouldn't send me money unless I had already depleted the previous month's budget. So, I would make up reasons not to keep the clothes bought for me. I had never lived with a sister before and I wanted to share with the other girls.

While I was in the group home, I colored Pam's hair for her, and helped with the cooking and cleaning. As you know by now, I had plenty of experience cleaning and doing chores, thanks to Dad.

I found a friend in Pam, and I loved her. She reminded me of my mother and was really wonderful. And Sherry was my soul sister at the group home—the little sister I never had. She was a big-time redneck, tough as nails. She was from St. Petersburg, the town where the group home was located. She never spoke about her parents, so for all I knew, she didn't have any.

Of the various activities we did, going to the beach was one of my favorites. One day, everyone from the group home went to St. Petersburg Beach and spent the entire day there. Pam's sister was dating Mike's brother, so they joined us as well. At the end of the day, everyone returned to the group home sunburned, tired, and happy.

I got into bed, exhausted and fell dead asleep. In the middle of the night, I awoke to find Mike's brother beside my bed, breathing on me. I was thirteen or fourteen years old and he was about twenty-four.

I was sleeping in a top bunk in my t-shirt and undies. He was standing next to my bunk, trying to get his hands under the covers. If I hadn't woken up, he probably would have gone as far as he could.

I thought, *Oh, my God! Not this again! I don't understand why this keeps happening to me.*

I tend to block things out as a coping mechanism. But as this guy was attempting to touch me, memories of the earlier molestations drifted back to me. The fact that it was happening a third time reinforced my feeling that I had done something wrong. I had a powerful sense of déjà vu.

I kept trying to keep my undies up and he kept trying to pull them down. I was embarrassed and worried that the other girls would wake up. I didn't want them to see what was happening and think I was a bad person. I thought they might think I'd invited the guy into my bed with me. I felt like I had to fix it. I had to get this guy away from me. So, I made exaggerated noises as if I were rolling over and waking up. It worked and the guy finally left.

I never told a soul. Like I said, I felt like I might have done something wrong, since this was the third time I had been molested. But I was determined not to let the molestations break me down. I was the same way when my dad used to hit me.

I made a plan to try to get moved into one of the rooms with a lock on the door. Space in those rooms was limited. Locked rooms were reserved for those who had been there the longest, were the most obedient, and did everything they were supposed to do. That was the rule: if you were really good, did your chores, obeyed the rules, and set goals for self-improvement, you could get a bed in one of those rooms.

I would end up getting moved into one of the locked rooms, but not until my last month there. That was the beginning of me learning to work the system. I was doing and saying whatever I had to do and say to get out of there.

While I was there, I was taught the three C's: cooperation, communication and control. I was there because I wasn't being cooperative at home. I figured out that if I cooperated, I would *get* my way or things would *go* my way. I felt strange, knowing that my self-improvement goals were coming from insincere motives. I felt like I was being manipulative. But I did what I had to do.

I would see the other girls doing something mischievous and getting into trouble, and I'd say to myself, *I'm not doing that! I don't want to be here longer or end up in an even worse place.*

When we had talk therapy, I made a point to participate—but speaking up still felt unnatural to me. My dad had trained me to feel like it was normal for him to bark orders at me—and abnormal or unnatural for me to speak up and try to explain myself. I had to teach myself to talk without fear of being punished for it.

These things were important, even though they seemed trivial at the time. Then one day, it really clicked. I said to myself, *I have to talk about things . . . communicate my feelings and opinions!*

I thought about how, when I was growing up, I was always being told, "Shut up, dummy!"

My childhood had taught me that the way to get my point across was to knock somebody down and fight. That's how I was treated and that's how I treated others. That seemed normal to me. Obviously, that is not how the world goes around, unless you are in prison or want to end up there.

I told myself that I had to be in control and not freak out. I had to work and play well with others—something that was outside my nature. I had to get along with a group of people, respect authority and stop making a big deal out of things. I stayed at the group home for three months and then graduated out of the system.

SEVENTEEN

B Y THE TIME I got out of the group home, Dad had been to
Minneapolis for his surgery at the Mayo Clinic and returned
home. Then we moved to a house on Saturn Avenue, a few miles
away from the Highland Avenue house. Luckily, we were close enough
that I got to keep most of my same friends. Most importantly, Debbie
and I remained friends, and she sometimes came to our parties.

There was a house on each side of our new house on Saturn Avenue.
The people who lived in the house on the left weren't particularly
friendly. The mom and daughters all wore long skirts and tennis shoes,
and had their hair up in buns. I thought they looked like Thanksgiving
pilgrims.

The minute I saw our new neighbors through the car windows, I
knew that Dad was going to have a field day with them. I thought to
myself, *Oh, my Lord, these poor people!*

I saw the writing on the wall. Dad was the type to mess with people,
laugh at them, mock them, and make fun of them. He would harass
people over their religion, their race—anything that struck him as
weird. He would make jokes at other people's expense, and call them
lesbians, rednecks, losers, and anything else that popped into his head.

Dad stalked and bothered those poor people to death. I never got to
know them so I couldn't say whether or not they were nice people. I do
know that they never bothered us, and they seemed like a good, kind
family.

Whatever Dad did, the neighbors turned the other cheek. They kept
to themselves, kept their heads down, and tried to stay out of Dad's

way. The man of the house was a tall, frail, wafer-thin woman of a man. He was no match for my beastly dad. Like his wife and daughters, the man put his head down and minded his own business.

Dad put transmission fluid in the carburetor. Then he backed up onto the neighbors' side of the driveway, almost all the way to their front door. He stepped on the gas while holding the emergency brake. Smoke poured from the exhaust pipe into the neighbors' house. They all came running out of the house, coughing.

Another time, Dad opened our windows and aimed the stereo speakers outside. The neighbors' house was only about twenty feet from ours, so they got blasted by the music.

While we were living in that house, my parents threw a big party and were out in the front yard with their guns. Both Mom and Dad had been drinking, and Dad had prescription drugs in his system, as always. Mom yelled at Dad to behave. Then Dad fired a shot into the air from the sawed-off shotgun he kept hidden in a cutout he made in the wall behind the T.V. (Dad always had a gun on him.)

One of the neighbors called the police and reported a disturbance. When the cops arrived, I realized I was going to have to be the adult and cover for them. I told the police that my parents were in bed, and I made up a story. I said that Dad had picked up a big stick in the front yard and was waving it around. I explained that it might have looked like a gun to the neighbors, being that it was dark outside and all.

By calling the police, the neighbors made my dad even more ornery than before. Now, he really went on the rampage. Those poor neighbors.

It was the across-the-street neighbors that finally took Dad's mind off our religious neighbors. They had kids around the same age as Ricky and me. These neighbors liked to party, and Dad loved his football parties. He would invite people over to watch the game on T.V., eat snacks and drink beer. These football parties were a big deal for dad.

Dad may have been a terror with our family, but he could be fun and sociable with friends when he set his mind to it. I never understood why he could be nice to friends when it suited him, and yet be so mean to my mom and us kids.

He slept in a hospital bed because of his back problems and Mom slept in their regular bed. Luckily for Dad, he was married to a woman who could function on very little sleep. So, when Dad woke Mom in the middle of the night for one reason or another, she could function.

She would sometimes have to get up at three in the morning to make my dad a fried baloney sandwich. He demanded all sorts of foods to satisfy the cravings he got from his different medications.

Dad set up an intercom system so he could plant himself in the back bedroom and yell into the intercom, "Laura!" His voice would echo throughout the entire house.

Even in front of company, he thought nothing of roaring, "Laura, get me a beer!"

It's disrespectful the way he treats Mom in front of other people, I said to myself. *He's always bossing her around.*

Mom took that treatment from Dad without saying anything. But it wore on her over time.

From time to time, Dad would get interested in a family activity. It would quickly turn into an obsession for him. Any time he got obsessed over something, we all had to participate—or else. For example, he decided that we should all collect sharks' teeth from the beach and make sharks-tooth necklaces.

Dad got all of us involved. He lined up the sharks' teeth and instructed us in the art of jewelry making. The plan was to make a bunch of necklaces and then sell them. Instead, Mom and Dad ended up giving them away.

The same thing happened when Dad got obsessed with ceramics. He soon had us all painting baked ceramic goods, with the idea that we would sell them. Then, every time a friend came over, he would give the pieces away. They never stuck with anything long enough to make it into a business.

(Speaking of sharks, my brother John was once hired by a fisherman to go out at night on a Styrofoam raft and chum the water for sharks. The fisherman could sell the meat for food and the teeth as a novelty. And, as I said, people like my dad would string the teeth into necklaces.

Intentionally trying to attract sharks to a Styrofoam raft sounded insane to me—but that was my brother. He was a wild and crazy guy, just like Dad. Not that Dad was John's bio-father, or mine for that matter.

In high school, I met Russell. He was a quiet bad-boy type who was in my same grade and either my age or a year older. He was tall and cute with brown hair. He didn't hang out with the jocks or the freaks, so he reminded me of myself. I did my own thing and never really belonged to any particular group. We both came from misfit families too, and we had that in common.

Russell and I fell head over heels in love and we dated for a long time. Then Dad had to go back to Minnesota for another back surgery and our family moved with him. We were only living in Minnesota for four to six months—but that was long enough for Russell to meet another girl.

That was the first time I had my heart broken. I couldn't understand how Russell could have been with another girl, especially considering how much he was calling me. He worked at the local country club and ran up an $800 bill on what was called the watts corporate line. (That was the line that employees used to make long distance calls.) He had to work extra hours to pay down the bill.

Now that I was back from Minnesota, I was willing to forgive and overlook Russell's cheating. He, on the other hand, wasn't as kindly disposed towards me. He didn't like the fact that I had less time for him than I had before I left for Minnesota. One of the things that was now keeping me busy was beauty pageants. (Mom had put me in modeling school when I was fifteen.)

Russell and I started arguing. We were not really getting along. One evening around dusk, when Russell dropped me off after spending the day together, we were arguing. I thought he was being controlling, and I didn't like it. And he thought that going to modeling school and doing beauty pageants was changing me, and *he* didn't like it.

I walked into the house, mumbling under my breath. I slammed the screened storm door loudly enough for Dad to hear all the way in the back bedroom.

Dad heard the commotion, came into the hallway, and looked my way. He was just in time to see Russell open the storm door and pull me outside to argue some more. The look on Dad's face was utter shock. Even though he was in his boxer shorts, overweight, and bloated from the surgeries and all the medications he was taking for his back, he came barreling down the hallway toward the front door.

I saw Dad reach into Ricky's room on his way to the front door, and grab a baseball bat.

"Oh, my God, Russell!" I yelled. "Let go of me! Get to your van! Go! My dad's gonna kill you!"

Russell sprinted to his van and hopped inside, with Dad in hot pursuit. Russell didn't even bother to the close the door. He tore out of there, tires squealing, before Dad could get to him. I'm sure that as Russell pulled away, he could see my dad, planted in the middle of the street with his baseball bat.

"You motherfucker!" Dad was screaming. "You'd better never come back here again!"

I thought for sure I was going to be in big trouble with my dad. Instead, he said to me, "Don't you ever let anyone touch you again!"

My dad had a saying for everything, but he didn't practice what he preached. He had stopped beating me, but that didn't mean I had forgotten all the beatings he had given me throughout my life. And I hadn't forgotten all the times he had put the fear of God into me with this warning: "Your mom brought you into this world. I can take you out."

Whenever Dad had threatened to kill me, I took him seriously. I knew he had killed before and I still remembered him slicing that man above the eye. I knew I was right to be afraid of him.

That was the last I ever saw of Russell. New boyfriends took his place. In fact, the phone never stopped ringing for me. And it always seemed to ring right as we sat down to eat, which really annoyed my dad. Not that we really ate together as a family much anymore. By now, we had all scattered to our own rooms and ate our meals alone.

The constant phone calls coming in for me irritated Dad to no end. Pretty much *everything* irritated him in those days, thanks to the effects of the Demerol and morphine he was taking for his back. It was really sad to see him suffering so much.

Dad never once talked about how badly his back was hurting, even though he was limping and obviously in terrible pain. But he did revert back to the days when he was really violent. Early in the morning one day, the phone rang. Since the calls were usually for me, I grabbed the phone, answered it, and stood there talking.

When I turned around, there was Dad. He was mad because the ringing of the phone had disturbed him, and mad because I was talking on the phone again.

He threw his coffee at me, but it wasn't hot anymore. It didn't burn me but it did scare me. Another time, he got so fed up, he ripped the phone clean out of the wall. It had to be replaced.

We all connected Dad's violent outbursts with his pain and tried to steer clear of him. The one person who couldn't really stay out of Dad's way was Mom. She functioned as his nurse and gave him his medication shots. (The Social Security office paid Mom to be Dad's disability nurse.) Dad would shout at Mom whenever he wanted something from her. He constantly had her scrambling around, trying to make him comfortable.

Living with constant pain wasn't just taking its toll on Dad's nerves; it was also affecting his appetite. He went through a phase where all he wanted to eat was pumpkin pie. The problem was, the medications he was taking would make him nod off while he was eating. We were all afraid he would suffocate when his head fell forward into his pie as he nodded off.

One time, I walked into Dad's room and found him nodded out with his face in his pie. He was burbling whipped cream out of his nose and he was on the verge of suffocating.

I had to grab the curly hair on the back of his head and pull him up out of the whipped cream. I started screaming for Mom and she ran in. Somehow, we got the whipped cream out of Dad's airways with our fingers.

Dad's constant pain also put him into a depression. Between the pain and the depression, Dad was in bad shape. The doctors even tried giving him shock treatments.

Eighteen

A ROUND THIS TIME, I met a guy named Lou who owned Lou's Tattoos. He was a tough New Yorker who had been friends with my dad for so long, we called him Uncle Lou. He knew that I liked to draw, so he put me to work in the tattoo shop.

I would answer the phone in the shop. And whenever somebody wanted a tattoo, I used my imagination to create a tattoo design for them. He would charge the customer a flat fee from the tattoo and give me some extra money in addition to my hourly wage.

A quiet, nice-looking young man named Al started hanging around the shop and eventually asked me out. We dated a little bit and have remained friends to this day. He was a few years older than me. He lost a leg after falling asleep while driving a motorcycle, and walked with a bit of a limp. When I quit working at the tattoo shop because I wasn't getting enough hours, I stayed friends with Al. He was like family.

I had traded in the hand-me-down Plymouth Sports Fury I'd been driving, and bought a Chevy Nova. Then a cute little convertible Triumph Spitfire caught my eye. So, I convinced Al to buy my Chevy Nova from me for seven hundred dollars. Then I used the money to buy my Spitfire. I felt like a million bucks driving that little car.

Now that I had the car of my dreams, I wanted my own place. A couple months later, I turned eighteen and moved into my own apartment in Clearwater.

Around that time, I found out that Dad had a little side hustle going on. When I saw a plastic bag filled with hundreds of pills, I put two and two together. I already knew how many different doctors Dad was seeing.

I decided to ask Mom about it. To my surprise, she told me what Dad was doing and how much he was making. He was selling his prescription pain meds to the tune of an extra $3,000 each month. Mom always talked to me about money. She wanted me to be very aware of where the money was coming from, and that it wouldn't be there forever.

Dad was already bringing in $2,000 a month between his Social Security Disability check, a Workman's Comp check and a settlement check from Butler Manufacturing. With this added pill-sales income, he was really raking in the dough. He was buying nice cars and scamming a few people along the way. Mom's sister, Aunt Peggy, and her husband fell victim to Dad's schemes.

Dad's pitch went like this: he was expecting a settlement and only needed some money until the check came in. As I said, the truth was that Dad was *already* drawing a disability check from the settlement. The settlement people were always trying to convince Dad to take a lump sum but he wouldn't do it.

I saw what Dad was doing and I didn't like it one bit. Some of these people Dad scammed were our friends. (And, of course, Aunt Peggy and her husband were family.) There was a guy at the junkyard who Dad helped with his cars. This guy's kids were our friends. It was one of the kids, in fact, who told me that my dad had scammed their dad out of some money.

The scheme with the man at the junkyard might have had something to do with the four-barrel Plymouth Sports Fury I mentioned owning. I used to race that Plymouth in drag races on the highway. I got paid sixty dollars for a win. The problem was, a speeding ticket was also sixty dollars. So, I quit racing, proud of the races I had won. Before I quit racing, I even took the car on a racetrack at Sunshine Speedway.

Dad built that car in the shop belonging to the junkyard owner. He used the guy's shop, his tools and probably some of the guy's auto parts. So, it was understandble that the junkyard owner felt that Dad owed him some money. Dad had worked on some other cars for the guy, and helped him around the shop. So, *he* felt that they were square.

After I quit working at the tattoo shop, I started working at McDonald's. Meanwhile, Al was working at the tattoo shop. One night, he decided to come pick me up from work. I had already told him that I had someone else picking me up and didn't need a ride home.

Mark, a popular super-jock from school, owned a black *Smokey and the Bandit* Trans Am. I had never seen such a cool car. So, when he asked me if I wanted a ride home from work that night, I thought, *Oh, my goodness! I have to ride in his car!*

I have always loved cars. Getting a chance to ride in the coolest car I'd ever seen was an invitation I couldn't pass up. To me, getting a ride home from work from this guy was no big deal. He drove me home and dropped me off.

A few days later, I saw Mark in the hallway at school. I said hi to him and he just ignored me.

"What's wrong?" I asked him.

Mark told me that after he dropped me off at my house, he drove to the beach. That was where all the kids hung out and parked. When he went to get out of his car, Al confronted him, saying something along the lines of, "What are you doing, giving my girl a ride home?"

Then Al pushed the car door on Mark's legs to intimidate him—but not hard enough to crush his legs. Mark's legs seemed okay to me.

Apparently, Al had waited at my workplace the night before, and seen Mark pull away with me inside his Trans Am. Al followed Mark to my house and watched him drop me off. And then he followed him to the beach.

I was really surprised when I found out what Al had done to Mark. I had never seen Al angry before. He was one of those quiet, charming types. I thought, *No wonder Mark wouldn't even say hi to me! Al must have put the fear of God into him.*

I decided that I had better switch Al from a boyfriend to a friend. I was pretty sociable and it wasn't unusual for me to have guy friends.

I couldn't have Al going around hurting any guy I happened to say hello to. As I said, Al and I remained friends over the years and are friends to this day.

I had been involved in modeling for a while by this point—ever since Mom got it into her head that this was a good idea.

"It's time for you to learn how to be a lady and stop being such a tomboy!" Mom said to me one day. She was bound and determined to make a lady out of me. So, she enrolled me in John Robert Powers Modeling school.

(My mother was ladylike in every way but one: she drove like a stunt driver. Watching her drive, I could hardly believe my eyes. She was always going the wrong way down one-way streets, swerving, and jumping over medians.)

I had a pageant coming up, and the entry fee was a couple hundred dollars. I wasn't thinking about the pageant when I jumped on my brother Ricky's motorcycle and took it out for a spin one day. But I started thinking about the pageant when I got in a wreck and got all skinned up.

"I can't be in the pageant now!" I said to my mom. "My legs are all torn up!"

"Oh, yes you can!" said Mom. "And you will!"

She made me walk down the runway with my skinned-up knees. We had already made plans for the pageant and invested in it, and I had made a commitment. She expected me to respect that.

Around the same time that I started modeling school, Dad started being a little aggressive toward my little brother. It all started when Dad thought Ricky was shooting glass in the backyard with a BB gun, and leaving the broken glass lying around.

Dad got angry and smashed the BB gun to pieces on the ground. He wouldn't listen to reason when we tried to explain that our dog was actually the culprit. He would chew pop bottles or whatever he could get his teeth into. Puppies don't understand that glass can hurt.

There was no way to talk to Dad and tell him that things weren't the way they seemed. He wouldn't hear it. He just reacted and lashed out.

Ricky was always a quiet little boy, and I felt very protective over him. He was four years younger than me and seemed more vulnerable. So, I always watched out for him.

He came up with a great way to escape the chaos of our household. He made a little reading hideaway for himself in his closet. He took his books in there and put them on a little shelf. He also dragged some pillows in there, along with a sleeping bag and a blanket. It was like a little fortress where he could tuck himself in and get away from it all.

Whenever things got too chaotic, and Ricky was missing, I'd find him hiding out in the closet, reading. When we got older, I asked him why he did that. He told me that he was scared and being in the closet made him feel safe. Also, reading was a great escape.

At the time, I worried about Ricky hiding out in his closet. I figured that unless he was tough like me and our brother John, he'd never survive. I knew I wouldn't always be around to look after him. Of course, what I didn't consider was the fact that our mom was quiet and graceful, like Ricky. He must have taken after her.

I felt that I needed to toughen up my little brother for his own good. I figured it was the only way he stood a chance in the world. I set out to teach Ricky to speak up for himself and become a fighter. I knew he'd need these skills for his survival.

One day, Ricky and I were bickering and he was calling me names. So, I pushed him through a storm door and into a concrete wall. He hit the wall so hard, he passed out.

John came running. When he saw Ricky lying there, he started yelling at me, "You killed him! You killed him!"

When Ricky got up, I jumped on top of him and started punching him.

"You're a bitch!" he said again and again.

Every time he called me a bitch, I punched him harder. I felt that he needed to learn that when you call someone a bitch out in the world, you'd better be ready for a throwdown. He had to learn to object to what someone was saying without calling them a bitch.

Ricky may have taken after our mom in his quiet ways—but he was also Dad's son. Like Dad, my brother was devious and mischievous, so, he rarely got caught causing trouble. He was Mr. Innocent. He would ride his motorcycle into the indoor parking garage of the Scientology building in downtown Clearwater, and steal motorcycle helmets and parts. He really aggravated the Scientologists.

Ricky rarely ran his mouth and was slow to react to taunts. That drove me crazy. I always knew how to aggravate John to get a rise out of him. I could get him to go from zero to crazy in three seconds. But I never could figure out how to get Ricky to react. I couldn't even beat it into him. He had a level of control over himself I had seen only in our mom.

Around this time, Ricky started to make himself scarce. He all but disappeared from our house. Technically, he still lived there but he had his own friends and pretty much lived his own life.

My parents weren't policing Ricky much as he got older. They were too lost in themselves. Ever since the shock treatments Dad had received for his pain and depression, he had been walking around like a zombie, bumping into walls. He was a shell of a person and only half there. He gained a lot of weight, and had to deal with strange food cravings and obsessions, like the pumpkin pie diet and the steak diet.

Meanwhile, Mom enrolled herself in a real estate course. Considering that Dad usually took up all of Mom's time, I don't know how she pulled it off. She even made a friend in the class—Angel, a former neighbor of ours.

Angel was a Greek woman, six feet tall with bushy, blonde-bombshell hair. She was busty and wore huge googly-eyed glasses with initials on the corner of the frames. Any time she walked into a room, everyone would stop and look at her. She was strong and independent. I thought she was beautiful.

Mom and Angel started going out and networking in the real estate community. Dad didn't like that at all. He was used to having a monopoly on Mom's time. The fact that Angel was single didn't help the matter any. Dad started calling Mom and Angel lesbians.

My parents started to drift apart and then suddenly they decided to remarry. The fact that they were unmarried at that time was news to me but not surprising. They tended to separate occasionally. Apparently, they went as far as divorcing, more than once. This was the third time they were going to remarry.

When it was time for the wedding ceremony, a justice of the peace came to the house and Mom and Dad renewed their vows. We were living in the house on Saturn at the time.

Meanwhile, the couple who lived across the street from us started to have troubles of their own. The wife started acting like she was getting ready to leave her husband. She hooked up with my dad's friend, Glenn. He had a glass eye and a weird sense of humor. He liked to tease us kids by taking out his glass eye and putting it in his beer.

The husband of the lady who was cheating with Glenn knew that Mom and Dad knew where his wife was, and what she was doing. So, he started calling our house, upset and crying, demanding to know, "Where's my wife?"

This went on for weeks. After a while, Dad got sick of it and started hanging up on the guy. One time when the husband of the cheater lady called, Dad was sleeping and Mom was out. So, I answered the phone. I could hear the man clicking his gun.

"I'm going to kill myself!" he said. "You'd better come over here and talk to me! I'm at the Orange Motel." The Orange Motel was at the end of our street.

Should I go over there? I asked myself. *I don't want him killing himself!*

I decided I'd better go over there and see if I could talk the man down. I was on my way out the door, headed over to the Orange Motel, when a friend distracted me. I went off with my friend and forgot all about the neighbor.

Later that night when I got home, I found out that the neighbor man had really done it. He had no one there to stop him and he took his life.

Oh, my God! I said to myself. *I forgot all about him! I should've gone and talked to him.*

When I told Mom about the neighbor man calling the house and asking me to come talk to him at the Orange Motel, she said, "It's a good thing you didn't go down there! It could've been dangerous."

"But I told him I was coming and then I didn't! I forgot!"

"No, Suzette. You did the right thing."

I thought about this man's kids no longer having a dad. I was also thinking about the blood in the motel room. From then on, I always thought of the Orange Motel as a sad, scary place at the end of our street.

The man's death left me feeling very sad, but I was still very young. I didn't stay focused on any one thing for very long. I forgot about the man as I got distracted by other things going on in my life.

Police Hold Man In Stabbing Case

Mother Of Two Wounded In Back

A man described by police as a rejected suitor was arrested late yesterday and accused of critically wounding a 22-year-old mother of two.

Mrs. Laura Poskar, 211 Linden Pl., underwent emergency surgery in Maumee Valley Hospital for a stab wound in her back.

Fred Duchoski, 30, of Flint, Mich., was booked in the Safety Building on a charge of stabbing with intent to kill or wound.

"I meant to kill her," Patrolmen Charles Diefenbach and Gerald Bedal quoted Duchoski as saying. The patrolmen said the suspect made the statement when he handed them a long-bladed steak knife as they entered the home.

The suspect, a race track groom, said the attack followed an argument with Mrs. Poskar, who is estranged from her husband. The patrolmen said Duchoski told them that he drove the knife into the woman's back by holding it with both hands.

Duchoski said the woman recently became friendly with another man, the policemen reported.

Article police holds man in stabbing

JUL • 60

Laura and first husband, John

Laura

Richard and baby Ricky

Laura and John, Jr.

Aunt Peggy

Grandpa Larry at
Cedar Pt. Amusement Park

Aunt Peggy as Gumdrop the Clown

Aunt Ethel as
"Secondhand Rose"

Grandma Tuttle

Great Aunt Mabel   Great-Aunt Mabel's mother

War ration book

Lawsie Tells Secret of Being 'Iron Man' at 76

By TONY WURZER

LAWSON (LAWSIE) WELCH has ICDABTY.
He is 76. Which makes it all the more remarkable.

Lawsie is a man the years have treated singularly lightly. His face is craggy. But not lined, like the old. And 76 is not young. It is a bronze face, like an Indian's. But Lawsie is Scotch-Irish.

"We're a hardy breed," he said smiling. He smiled a lot. When he does, he reveals two big, gleaming gold teeth. All the rest are his own and original.

He stripped off his checkered shirt, pounded on a chest, filled with muscles and pink and firm, like a young man's.

"I challenge any man in the world," Lawsie said. "Age makes no difference. If he weighs 145 pounds, I challenge him. And, if he beats me, he wins a brand new, polished, gleamin' gorgeous $6000 automobile. And that's the truth."

Lawsie stopped in Buffalo today long enough to visit his daughter, Mrs. Otto Regensdorfer, 27 Mariner St.

There, in the dimly lit, tiny little front room, Lawsie showed some of his remarkable talents. He is a physical marvel. At 76 he is like Bernarr Macfadden used to beat 60.

He's from Ashtabula, O. In that area, and through Pennsylvania and the other states around Ohio, Lawsie is known as the Ohio Wonder; the Ageless Man; the Man Most Likely to Live Forever.

He will lift 100 pounds 100 times. He will swing Indian clubs seven different ways for more hours than the average guy can stand. He will punch the bag, simultaneously, with his head, elbows,

knees, fists, and keep them rattling like ack-ack. He will do a press-up 100 times. He will exercise 1200 different ways with a 12-pound dumbell.

And, if that isn't enough, he will wrestle you.

If you beat him at these things, a man named Joe Cimorell of 3018 Blair Ave., in Ashtabula, will gladly hand you that $6000 auto.

Lawsie is a friendly man. He's about 5-7, weighs 170 pounds now. Sixty years ago the doctors told him he would not live long. Bad pump.

"I found the cure—exercise," Lawsie explains.

"I believe a man must be active to live long and soundly," Lawsie said. "The body is a machine that builds itself up with exercise. Muscles, tissues grow. But they must be broken down first. They can't be broken down by sitting."

Lawsie helps nature along a little. He doesn't smoke, or drink.

"I eat one can of spinach every day, just like Popeye; eat a couple of eggs, a lot of fruit and see that I get eight, nine hours of sleep," he says. "That's all there's to it."

"ANOTHER thing," he yelled, still keeping the sledge twirling like a propeller. "Tell 'em to quit looking for a knock in the human motor. Tell 'em to learn to like work, like people, laugh and learn to accept knocks. Tell em, most of all, to laugh. Some people bust their faces when they laugh, they're so unused to it."

Oh, the ICDABTY?

That means I Can Do Anything Better Than You.

LAWSIE WELCH
At 76 He's Found Secret of Health

Iron Man, age 76

Great-grandpa Lawsie Welch

Great-grandpa Lawsie Welch

Great-grandpa Lawsie Welch

Laura and Richard
at the Midway Inn

1977—Richard at home

Greg and Suzette

Grandma Margaret

Suzette

Sherry from the group home

Suzette and Debbie from jr. high

Bobby and Donna's family

Andy and Suzette

Suzette and Debbie
from high school

1991—Suzette and Debbie from high school

Julie at Ollie's Bar

Tattoo Al

Laura

Nancy and Laura

House on Saturn St.

1967 Plymouth Sports Fury

Suzette with pixie
given by Laura

1970 Suzette sneaking a snack

1971 Suzette in Jack and
Inez's backyard

Elementary school picture

Elementary school picture

PRESENTER:

Suzette Shanle

A fun, energetic educator, well-known for her inventive concepts in haircutting and fitting clients with looks to suit their faces, shapes and profiles. This inventor of the spaz perm will help you get in touch with your creative side.

Suzette teaching
hair techniques to stylists

Suzette Shanle artwork to be displayed at Wesleyan University

LINCOLN — The artwork of Suzette Shanle of Genoa will be on display Feb. 24 through March 15 at the Elder Gallery on the Wesleyan University campus in Lincoln.

Shanle

The artwork is part of a 67-piece display entered into an art competition with artists from around the state.

Shanle attends Wayne State College, and will graduate this spring with a bachelor's degree in art education.

She is a former student of Richard Abraham, art instructor at Central Community College-Columbus.

Suzette's artwork article

Jon Paul Shanle and
John Paul De Jorria

Suzette and John Paul De Jorria

1991 Trans Am

Pageant article revealing address

Modeling shot

High school senior picture

High school senior picture

Modeling for bridal show

Mr.& Mrs.DANNIE B.ARMSTRONG,Owners **TRAVELIN GAMBLER** DAMAXIM JUNIOR.........2nd.
DANNIE B. ARMSTRONG,.Trainer   WHIRL O'LIVING.....3rd.
J. R. DONLON.........Jockey   6/7/86   27.80   11.40   5.80
6 Furlongs   1:17.3 Muddy track - $2,500 Claiming-Ne.Bred-Exacta $174.50-Purse $1200

Laura and J.R. winning at racetrack

Suzette's family after Columbus flood

OFFICE OF THE VICE PRESIDENT
WASHINGTON

April 26, 1990

Ms. Suzette Renee Poskar
2903 21st Street
Columbus, Nebraska 68601

Dear Suzette:

    Thank you for all of your assistance during my recent visit
to Columbus. I know that you devoted a lot of time and energy on
my behalf to ensure a successful trip, and I am grateful for your
supportive efforts.

    With best wishes, I am

                    Sincerely,

                    Dan Quayle

OFFICE OF THE VICE PRESIDENT
WASHINGTON, DC

VICE PRESIDENT

Thank you letter from White house

V.P. Dan Quayle and Governor Kay Orr

1996—Suzette and Terry wedding

Laura and J.R. wedding

Suzette and Laura

Nineteen

John started working at Maddox roofing. I also went to work there part-time as a receptionist. I was on the tail end of fifteen years old, so I was working under the table. One day when the phones were slow, I was flipping through a teen magazine and saw an ad for the Miss National Teen pageant.

I decided to send in my photo and registration. I had to write an essay and submit some other information, as well. Once I had sent in my information, I forgot all about it. The next thing I knew, I received a letter stating that I was chosen to be Miss Clearwater in the Miss National Teen pageant.

I was really excited about it. At first, I didn't even tell Mom about me being Miss Clearwater. When I finally did tell her, she said. "Suzette, you have to do this in a responsible way. You represent this town now and you have to do a good job!"

A press release was sent to the media and that led to the local newspaper sending a reporter to our house to write an article about me. As I was answering the reporter's questions, I was blunt and honest, as usual. I talked about my overdose at twelve years old—and the paper decided to devote an entire page to me and my drug use.

I told the reporter, "Back when I was twelve, I had some trouble. But that was a long time ago. I'm in a really good place now!"

The reporter twisted my words to sensationalize it. They were looking for a "Teen Goes from Drug Use to Beauty Pageant" kind of headline. That's what they created, by twisting my words around.

The article claimed that I had used cocaine, but that was a flat-out lie. I had never even heard of cocaine. I was mad and hurt over that. All I had tried to do was enter a teen beauty pageant and now they were making up lies about me.

I was crushed. I figured, *Well, that's the last time I'll ever trust anyone to write an article about me!*

Having a write-up on me in the local paper gave me a lot of exposure. The phone started ringing with friends congratulating me on being chosen Miss Clearwater. Unfortunately, all that exposure also led to me having my very own stalker.

One time when the phone rang, I answered it and heard a guy breathing heavily. He used a real muffled, freaky voice and kept saying my name over and over again. The first time it happened, I thought one of my friends was messing with me and I hung up on the guy.

Then he called again, later the same day. This time, his voice was clear. I had grown up fighting with boys, so this guy didn't scare me. I thought, *Oh, please . . . is this guy kidding me?* And I hung up on him.

The third time the guy called that day, he was talking very slowly, so he could keep me on the phone longer. I have always had superhuman hearing—like a dog—and I heard something interesting in the background. There was the sound of pots and pans clanging.

Oh, this guy's at work, I said to myself. *He must work in a kitchen. I wonder how he's managing to call me from work.*

To make matters worse, the guy had our family's name and address. He got it from the article about me.

The stalker started calling our house at all hours of the day and night. He would say things like, "I know what you're doing and where you've been."

On one call he said, "I know what you wore today—a pink shirt. And you had a white purse." He was very specific and frighteningly accurate. (This was in the days before cell phones.)

These calls went on for weeks, maybe even months. I would walk in the door of the house, hear the phone ringing, and answer it. Then I would realize it was my stalker, and hang up on him. When someone else in my family answered the phone, they hung up on him.

These calls freaked out my mom even worse than me. In looking back, I think she might have thought it was Fred. She got very jumpy and hypervigilant.

At some point, I realized I was going to have to change my strategy if I had any hope of shaking the guy. Now when he called, I talked to him. Like my mom, I'm a fixer. I thought that maybe I could help the guy understand that whatever he thought was going on between us was a figment of his imagination. My hope was that I could help him get over his obsession with me and then move on and leave me alone.

From the sound of his voice, I figured he was somewhere between thirty and forty. That seemed old to me at the time. It creeped me out to think of this old man stalking me.

It was strange to feel totally creeped out by the stalker but empathetic toward him at the same time. I connected the stalker calling all the time with the neighbor who started out calling our house asking for his cheating wife, and ended up killing himself. Knowing that the neighbor had killed himself made me want to try to help the stalker.

I would say to myself, *This poor person! He really needs to move on and put his attention on his real life. He shouldn't be spending all his free time calling me—a stranger!*

I tried to draw out the stalker by asking him questions. One time I was asking him a question when Dad came around the corner and heard me. He snatched the phone out of my hand, saying, "You're going to get yourself hurt! Do not say one word to him ever again."

I knew that Dad was right. The stalker really *could* have hurt me. Being young and inexperienced, I wasn't taking the guy as seriously as I should have. My parents definitely knew the potential danger the guy posed.

Mom took me to the Clearwater Police Station. She thought maybe they could help us get rid of the stalker. We went inside and were directed to the desk of one of the detectives. The area where the detectives sat was way in back. On all three of the desks, folders were piled up in a haphazard way.

Wow, these detectives are a mess! I thought. I had grown up with

Dad's insistence that everything always be spic-and-span. He ruled with an iron fist and a white glove.

When we were seated at the desk of one of the detectives, he asked us what the problem seemed to be.

"Some man keeps calling my daughter and following her around," explained Mom.

"How did he get your name and number?" asked the detective.

Mom explained about me entering the beauty pageant, and about the article being written about me.

The detective reached over and picked up one of the files off his desk. Then he opened it and showed me and my mom a photo of a lady lying on the floor. She was dead, with a phone cord wrapped around her neck.

"You see this?" he said. "Well, this is what happened to one woman who had a stalker calling her!"

He closed that file and picked up another one. "And you see this one?" he said, showing us a photo of a lady with a bloody head. "She's another one."

When Mom saw me cover my eyes, she said to the cop, "What the hell are you doing?"

I knew that Mom must have been really upset for her to curse. She felt that the detective should have talked to her without me present. She didn't want him scaring me.

"I want you to know this is serious!" he said. "Unfortunately, there are laws governing prosecution of these offenses. This man has not threatened you right?" he asked me.

"No..."

"And you've never seen him, right?"

I said that no, I hadn't seen him.

"Well, the way the laws are written, we can't do anything until he threatens you or hurts you. In fact, until we know who this person is, we can't even talk to him."

"You mean to tell me that you can't help us?" asked Mom.

"The only thing you can do is stop answering the phone! And change your phone number!"

Walking into my house had always felt safe to me for one reason: my parents were armed! There were baseball bats behind doors and guns on shelves. And Mom slept with a big knife under the mattress.

Given that Mom had been stabbed so badly when I was young, I totally understood why she slept with a butcher knife. And as for Dad having guns in the house, I understood that too. Dad was always paranoid that someone might come looking for him over his scams.

When we left Ohio years earlier, Mom worried that Dad might have stolen money while running numbers. She figured that might be the reason he made himself scarce. Dad was secretive about a lot of things. Since he wouldn't say one way or another what had happened, we were left to figure things out. I assumed that he had gotten himself mixed up with the mob somehow.

When we got home from the police station, Dad came out of his room. It was unusual for him to get up but this time, he came and sat down at the table.

I went into my room and let my parents talk it out. I had seen a dead body in that photo, and that had scared me. It was a reality check. When you put your name out in the world because you want to be known for something, it seems so innocent. But sometimes your wish comes true, and you're known alright—by the wrong people.

I was being stalked and I could have died. That was the reality. I walked over to the window and busied my mind. I wondered what the man in the moon was doing that night. That kept my mind off the gruesome photos. I have always had a way of blocking out things that are bad. The man in the moon was a big help in that department.

Our whole family started following a strict routine of going to work, coming home, going to school, and coming home. The police felt that the less time we spent in public, the less exposed we would be, and the less chance there would be of anything happening to me. My parents kept me close.

After seeing those gruesome photos, I had no problem with that routine. Normally, I liked to be out and about. Knowing I could really be in danger, I was willing to spend more time at home.

Dad said, "There's no way I'm changing my fucking phone number for no psycho!" So, the calls continued coming in.

I wasn't allowed to answer the phone anymore. So, now when the stalker called, he got someone else in my family. Everyone in my family started saying I wasn't home unless the person calling was someone they knew.

I thought, *This man must have no life! He's so bored!*

One night right before the time I was due to get off work, the stalker called the house. He said, "I know that Suzette is working at Charlie's Steakhouse and I know what time she gets off. I'm going to get her!"

Al and I had remained friends and he happened to call the house that night. When Dad talked to Al, he figured it would be good to tell him what was going on. That way, Al might be able to get to Charlie's before my parents did and protect me from the stalker.

Since these two calls had come in while I was already at work, I had no way of knowing about the stalker planning to come get me. I didn't know that Dad had sent Al on ahead either. On that particular night, I was working as the hostess and I was the one closing.

Around 9:45 or 10:00, I closed Charlie's and got ready to go home. Being the last one there, I had no one to walk me to my car. I usually parked way at the back of the parking lot because the lot tended to be full by the time I arrived for work. So, I had a little ways to walk.

The completely empty parking lot was the size of a football field. The walk to my car seemed endless that night, and my heart started beating fast. I was almost to my car when a car started coming right toward me with its headlights on. As I looked at that car, a second car appeared, and started coming at me as fast as it could.

I froze, petrified. As I said, I had no idea that the stalker had threatened to come after me that night. All I knew was that these two cars seemed to be coming right for me. I watched the cars speed up alongside me—one on one side, one on the other. When they got close enough, I could see mom and dad in one car and Al in the other. I've never been so relieved in my life!

That was the end of me working at night. To this day, I have no idea whether my stalker was also there that night. He could have been hiding somewhere in the dark and watching Al and my parents show up to protect me. Maybe he realized he would be unable to get at me and moved on to someone else.

All I know for sure is that the stalker never called again after that night. "I hope he's in prison. Or dead," said Dad.

It was a long time before my family and I let our guards down again.

TWENTY

I was always very quiet and shy. I didn't know many people at Clearwater High School, and I had very few friends. I wasn't doing great academically either. I was getting low test scores in my classes. I had never been good at school and had always struggled through it.

The guidance counselor asked me what I wanted to do or be when I got out of school. Being Miss Clearwater and having to look pretty and ladylike with styled hair and nice makeup had renewed my interest in becoming a hairdresser.

I had *always* been interested in becoming a hairdresser. Hearing stories of both my grandmother and my mother being hairdressers pushed me in that direction, and gave me confidence. It also made me feel like I was carrying on the family tradition.

One day while I was trying to figure out what I wanted to do with my life, I was sitting on the floor in front of the mirror in the hallway, trying to curl my hair just right.

Dad saw me sitting there, and yelled down the hall, "She has to go to beauty school! She's always in the mirror!"

I told the guidance counselor that I was interested in becoming a hair stylist. So, they put me in the work experience program. I went to Dunedin School for cosmetology and auto shop class. And I continued to attend Clearwater High School for all my other classes. I was driving back and forth between the two schools.

Clearwater High was a big school, so they split up the students into two shifts. Some of us went to school from 7:00 in the morning until 11:00, and some started school at 11:00 in the morning and got out at

3:00. (I was in tenth grade by now.) I started out in first shift and then earned my spot in the second shift.

Around the time I started attending Dunedin High School for my cosmetology classes, Ricky started skipping school altogether. He was in the seventh grade at the time. Mom got a shock when the principal from Ricky's school called to let her know that she needed to come down to the school. He told her that my little brother had only been to school a few days in the entire semester.

Apparently, Ricky's I.Q. test revealed that he had a college-level I.Q. So, being in junior high with that kind of intellect left him bored to death. Socially, he felt like he was on a totally different level. So, he had no interest in that aspect of school either.

Ricky had two parents with great genes, intelligence-wise. I figured out how smart Dad (Ricky's bio-father) was when I found an engineering book for a class he was taking. I had never seen such complicated math equations.

Both Ricky and John quit school in the seventh grade. It was a battle of wills, and Mom finally said, "Okay, go to work if you're not going to go to school. Just do what you're going to do and do a good job at it."

I was totally freaked out and seriously pissed. I was thinking, *Wait a minute . . . here I am stuck in school, fighting for C's, and my brothers get to quit school?*

When John quit school, he went to work at a roofing company. He had taken construction classes at school, and that experience made it easy for him to learn how to do roofing.

Before getting the roofing job, John worked for a garbage company. One day, Mom and I took the family VW to pick up John from work. It was a smoldering hot day. When my brother got into the car, he was so stinky, I almost got sick. There's nothing worse than the combination of garbage and intense heat. I couldn't figure out how he stood that kind of work. But I knew he made three times more money than he would in a regular job, so I got it. Money was always a big motivator for me too.

Meanwhile, I was real busy driving back and forth between schools in my Spitfire. I also kept myself busy dating different boys.

A boy asked me out to lunch and I thought, *Sure. Why not?* So, I agreed.

The guy arrived while I was still getting ready for our lunch date. He was sitting outside waiting for me in his black 1969 Pontiac Grand Prix.

When I went outside to meet him, he was bleeding from his face and peeling away in reverse.

I turned around and saw my brother John standing there. "What happened?" I asked him.

"He looked like Jesus . . . so I had to punch him in the face."

I had to admit that John was right. The guy was tall and thin with long hair like Jesus. That was John. If he thought you looked weird, he wouldn't think twice about laying you out.

One day around this time, I came out of my room just in time to see paramedics putting my mom on a stretcher and wheeling her down the hallway.

Dad must have found Mom unresponsive and decided that it was better if we kids stayed in our rooms until the paramedics got her into the ambulance. If I hadn't come out of my room and seen them wheeling Mom down the hallway, God knows when Dad would have told me what had happened. He never was one to say much.

Mom stayed gone only a day or so. While she was gone, it somehow came out that she had tried to kill herself. I knew that Mom was very unhappy with having to stay home and be Dad's nurse, especially since the medications he was taking made him so emotionally distant from her.

Dad's back troubles led to depression and psychological problems. Then his medication came into the picture and caused even more problems. Since Mom was Dad's caretaker and at his beck and call, his physical condition had a major effect on her. Mom was a fixer of other people's problems. When it came to her own problems, she tried not to put anyone out. She was tough like that.

One time I woke up in the middle of the night and found Mom standing at the stove, making a fried baloney sandwich for Dad. Her eyes were closing on her because she was half asleep. She reached over to the sink, grabbed the squeeze bottle of dish soap instead of the bottle of cooking oil, and squeezed some into the pan.

"Mom! What are you doing?"

Mom had obviously been sleep-cooking. I didn't even know there was such a thing until then. When Mom heard my voice, she startled awake.

"Dad will kill you if you give him that sandwich!" I said.

She dumped it in the trash and started all over.

There had never been enough of Mom to go around. Dad demanded too much of her time. I could see the cumulative effect it had on my mother. I think she felt like she was losing herself in all the chaos and becoming invisible. She put all her energy and focus into taking care of Dad, which left no room in her life for herself.

When you spend your entire life doing things for other people and never have time for yourself, that's what happens. You lose yourself and your own personal identity starts to disappear.

I had seen Mom changing right before my eyes. She had always been a woman who took time with her hair and makeup and looked beautiful. Then she started putting on weight because she was stuck in the house with Dad all the time.

When Mom came home from the hospital, our routine went right back to normal. And no one said a word about what had happened. But Mom started living her life in a different way after that. Now, she focused more on the real estate courses she'd been taking.

I think taking courses was Mom's way of taking baby steps toward better self-care. I'm sure the courses made her feel better about herself. By then Dad was so out of it, he couldn't object.

One day when Mom was getting ready to go to class, she was standing in front of the mirror in the one little bathroom we all shared.

"Suzette," she said, "remember, it's just as easy to fall in love with a rich man as a poor man."

She had said that to me before, and I never understood what she was getting at. I thought to myself, *Okaaay! Whatever that means! I don't want to get married anyway.*

I understood that Mom was talking about *her* husband as much as she was cautioning *me* about what to look for in a future husband. And I knew that, even though Dad brought in money, the way he treated Mom wasn't anywhere near as good as the way she treated him.

I knew that Dad was in terrible pain, and I hated to see him go through that. It was horrible. But I didn't feel that Dad's pain was an excuse for the way he treated Mom.

She deserves better, I said to myself.

I wanted my mom to be happy. So, any time we would drive over railroad tracks, I would lift my feet and make a wish that I had a million dollars to give to her. (I'm not sure where I got that lifting of the feet and making a wish on railroad tracks habit, but there you have it.)

First Mom got so fed up with her life, she tried to kill herself. Then she started trying to become more independent with her real estate courses. Next, she started defying Dad. Instead of staying at home at Dad's beck and call, Mom was suddenly going shopping, or out to bars to have a few drinks with Angel after their real estate class.

For once, my mother had a friend, and Dad wasn't having it. He resented having to give himself his own shots and do things for himself as Mom got busier. In her real estate class, my mother also met the mom of Nancy, a classmate of mine. Nancy and I hung out together and liked to go roller skating.

Nancy's mom started coming to our house for football parties. Uncle Greg remained a fixture in our lives during this time, as well. One night, we all stayed up late, partying, and Nancy's mom had so much to drink, she found herself in bed with Greg. In the morning, she came out of the spare room, looking like a wreck. She was totally embarrassed.

As school came to an end, the cosmetology school I attended occasionally hired me to come back and teach styling and cutting techniques to the class of younger girls.

When I was in 10th grade, I attended John Robert Powers Modeling School for a year. Then I won a scholarship to Barbizon Modeling School in Tampa. I took a few classes there. I felt like everything I was learning had already been covered at John Robert Powers. So, I didn't stay long at Barbizon.

Around this time, Grandma Margaret moved back to Florida after living in Minnesota near Aunt Peggy. She rented a condo at Morningside Apartments, and was now across town from us. She would often come over on weekends, take a seat in a chair, and sit there reading a book. I loved her and really enjoyed her being there. Dad never raised his voice when Grandma was present.

TWENTY-ONE

B Y NOW, MY figure was developing. I noticed that boys were starting to look at me differently. Older guys were looking at me too, which was creepy. Mom's wish had come true and I had become more girly and less of a tomboy. I wore my hair very blonde and was doing beauty pageants.

I was a little bit nervous about the Miss National Teen Pageant, but it turned out to be pretty uneventful. Dad didn't like being around people, but he sucked it up and walked me onstage.

There was no talent portion of the pageant, and that was fine with me. I was grateful that I didn't have to speak in front of a crowd. I did have to sit at the judge's table and answer questions, though. I always had Dad's voice in my head, calling me a dummy. And I never forgot that I didn't seem to speak properly.

I had gotten a couple of sponsors for the pageant. A sponsor was someone who bought an ad in the pageant program. Those sponsors purchasing ads led to me having my photo on more pages in the program and earning extra awards. My sponsors were Tattoo Al, State Farm (where Mom once worked), and Doc and Bill's Junkyard. (Doc sponsored me before he and Dad had their falling out.)

I thought to myself, *Well, I did it! I'm so glad it's over now.*

For my sixteenth birthday party, we had a keg of beer. Word got out about the party and people started showing up. The crowd included friends of my parents and friends from some of the different neighborhoods where we had lived. Both of my friends named Debbie were there. One was a friend from junior high and the other was my best friend from high school. A neighborhood guy named David Long and his sisters, Cathy and Judy, were also there.

There were a lot of kids around my age in our neighborhood and they started showing up too. Pretty soon, our house filled up with people. We had over a hundred cars parked up and down my road. The house was alive and breathing with people, and we were having so much fun.

I like parties but I am generally uncomfortable when there are too many people around. I get overstimulated. But I knew everybody there and had known them forever. So, I had a great time. So did everyone else. In fact, people had so much fun, they still talk about it today.

Toward the end of the night, my friend Teddy had too much to drink and punched a hole in the wall of our house. In the moment, no one thought too much of it. Many people slept over, sprawled out all over our house, too wiped out to drive home. The next morning when Teddy woke up, he tried to creep out the door.

Dad had wakened up before Teddy and intercepted him as he was sneaking out the door. Handing him a bucket of spackle, Dad said to Teddy, "Sir, I think you've got some spackle work to do before you leave."

Dad was huge and Teddy was on the smaller side. So, all he said was "Yes, sir!"

Teddy was still green around the gills from all his partying the night before. But he took Dad seriously and fixed the hole in the wall. Then he went to leave.

"I think you'd better put a little bit more on," said Dad. "You're going to have to wait until that dries, sand it, and then add some more spackle."

All in all, it took Teddy about two hours to repair the wall.

Dad wasn't mad at Teddy. He of all people knew that when people drank, stuff happened. As I got older, he started being nicer to my friends. He seemed to have calmed down a bit. I couldn't say whether that was due to his medication or the fact that he was now seeing a therapist.

I had met some new friends when they came to my sixteenth birthday party, including the Perkins family from Boston who lived down the street. Having more good people around was making me feel better about my life.

After I turned sixteen, Dad bought a boat—an awful, ugly, twenty-footer. I thought the boat was a mess, but Dad was excited about his new fix-it project. He had never owned a boat before and was happy to have one.

Dad recruited all of us to help him fix up the boat, and Uncle Greg too. We kids were in charge of sanding the boat so Dad could apply a coat of primer. Dad and Greg took care of all the electrical issues, fixing and updating all the knobs and mechanical buttons.

Then, he had the boat professionally painted. Meanwhile, Mom was using a special machine to reupholster the seats. By the time she was done with the seats, they were white with blue piping and looked beautiful. I wasn't too surprised by that. After all, Mom had sewn my clothes when I was younger.

When all was said and done, the entire boat was absolutely beautiful. Sometimes we would launch our boat in Largo and head over to the Tampa Bay causeway. I loved taking the boat out on the weekends and having fun—but I didn't like the coming back part. I hated emptying the boat when I was tired from a day of boating, and all the spraying and scrubbing that went into cleaning it.

One time, Mom, Dad, Ricky, my friend Nancy and I went boating, along with Uncle Greg. He was now single and spent a lot of time at our house on the weekends. He was really present in our lives and spent a lot of time with Dad, which was fine with me. He was casual and fun.

We went island hopping that day, making stops at Honeymoon Island and John's Pass. These were places where we could drive the boat onto the beach, dock it, and spend the day. We were the only ones on the island. We had so much fun.

We made a grill by digging a firepit in the ground and ate the food we had brought from home. We explored the island and looked for shells. Dusk kind of crept up on us. Suddenly we realized we'd better get our things together and start to head home. The only thing was, the tide had gone out. Now we were stuck. The boat was in water too shallow for us to get out.

Dad was strong but he really needed some help. Ricky was still pretty little and not very strong yet. Greg didn't have legs that functioned in the way that he could have helped push the boat out into the water. He could move fast on his crutches, probably faster than any of us, but he didn't have the leg strength to push the boat. (You might remember that he had developed his upper body strength well enough that he was able to swim. He was the one who taught me how to swim.)

As it got darker, we realized we might have to spend the night on the island. We knew that in the morning, the tide would come back in. We could get off the island then. In the meantime, we had no choice but to make the best of it.

The idea of spending the night on the island didn't sit well with Dad. He started getting crabby. There didn't seem to be anything we could do. We sat there on the beach and watched the other boats buzzing by, knowing we were stranded. The boats were too far out to notice us sitting there, watching them.

We built a little fire and hung out—but we were uncomfortable. Our clothes and towels were damp from being out in the water all day. Eventually it got really dark and miraculously, the tide came back in. It was very late at night by then. The good news was that the tide had come in enough for us to get the boat afloat again. The bad news was that we were now in a boat in pitch blackness.

Dad was new to boating. He had never taken the boat out in the dark before. So, it was tricky for him and scary for the rest of us. I kept feeling like we were going too fast. That might have been because I was thinking about the fact that I've never been a very good swimmer. As we got close to home, Dad used the lights along the shoreline to navigate the boat into the dock.

We were close to shore and just about feeling relieved because we'd made it home without any disasters. Then, Dad scraped the underside of the boat on something. We heard a big bang and lurched forward. The boat didn't take on water. It was able to keep going, but slower than before.

When we made it home and got out to survey the damage, we saw that the boat had a big dent and scrape on it. It was a shame after all the time our family had spent fixing up the boat.

Dad worked on repairing the boat, but we never took it out again. I don't know whether he felt unsure about the repairs he'd made or lost his feeling for boating. Either way, that was the end of our adventures in the S.S. Minnow.

One day, Mom told me, "You know, the doctor says Richard is a narcissist."

I would later look back and realize that this was the moment when Mom started to give up on Dad. When a professional told Mom that Dad was a narcissist, I think she realized she would never be able to fix him.

I had no idea what the word narcissist meant. All I knew was that it was hard for me to have sympathy for someone who had been so mean to me in the past. When Mom said that to me, I thought, *Call him any doctor thing you want! I have no sympathy for him.*

When I was little, all I had to do was walk past Dad and he would hit me upside the head. It was shocking—and random. I would be walking by, minding my own business, and *bam!*

Dad had mostly stopped hitting me by the time Mom told me what the doctor said about Dad. I was glad—but feeling sympathy toward him was still hard for me.

Mom had passed her real estate course and now she had some time to spend shopping with me for pageant clothes. She and Dad were also going to open houses in their spare time. Then Dad started taking a college course himself.

One day, I saw one of my dad's textbooks from the class, and it was open. There was a math problem that took up the entire page. I didn't usually think of my dad as being smart in that way. I knew he was mechanical and could fix things around the house. But I didn't realize he could do the kind of advanced math problems that engineers do.

When I asked Mom about it, she said, "Your dad's very intelligent!"

It seemed like all of us were now doing our own thing. John was doing construction and roofing and had moved down the road, where he was living with a buddy of his. Ricky was working as a mechanic, and was usually off running around with his friends. He was often working on motorcycles or bicycles, and coming home with spare parts for his bikes. Dad had bought Ricky a Yamaha 80, which he had taken apart and put back together.

One day, I walked up to the porch to go inside the house and saw Ricky's Yamaha 80. It was just sitting out front. I jumped on the bike, turned the key and went flying down the street. I was fearless. I didn't know how to ride it, but I had seen the boys ride their motorcycles hundreds of times.

I approached a four-way stop. A car suddenly appeared and scared me half to death. I had no idea how to slow the bike down or downshift, so I did the only thing I knew how to do. I tilted my body to the side and lay the bike down. I got a terrible road rash on the left side of my body—my elbow, my hip, my leg, the whole left side of my body.

I hadn't been going that fast at the time, but I was going fast enough to get pretty bruised and scraped up. I had also scratched up my brother's bike. I jumped up, thankful that I wasn't dead. I shook off the pain, looked around and realized no one had seen me lay down the bike.

I pushed the bike home and left it in front of the house where I found it. Then I went inside and cleaned myself up. That was a pageant weekend and now I was all bruised and scraped up.

It had cost Mom $300 for me to be in the pageant and $150 for the dress. And there was no guarantee I would win any money, either. Sometimes I did win awards and prizes but winning wasn't my goal. I was just trying to get more comfortable in front of people. I had such terrible stage fright.

The day before the pageant, I was wearing a long-sleeve shirt.

"Suzette, it's too hot to be wearing that shirt! Take it off."

"I can't."

"What do you mean you can't? Why not?"

I had never told my mom a lie since one time when I was little and stole some jewelry and nail polish from Woolco.

"I can't lie to you, Mom. I dropped Ricky's motorcycle and now I'm all scratched up."

"Oh, Suzette! How scratched up?"

I took off my shirt and showed her my left arm.

"Is there more?"

"Yes," I said. I was wearing shorts, so all I had to do was turn my body and she could see all the damage I had done to the left side of myself. The scrapes and bruises went all the way down to my ankle and extended even to my feet. I never did like proper shoes and had been wearing sandals while riding Ricky's motorcycle.

My mom was the sweetest lady you would ever meet. I knew her heart went out to me—but she was also tough.

"Listen, Suzette, I'm sorry. I feel bad that you've had this injury. But you need to fulfill your obligations. We paid all this money and you've been practicing for the pageant! So, you're going, injured or not."

So, that's what I did. We made the forty-five-minute drive to Tampa, and I went through with it. Mom had me wear dancer pantyhose with my swimsuit to cover my injuries. She also made me a shawl to drape over my injured shoulder. I put my injuries out of my mind and competed as if nothing was wrong with me.

I won third place. Al even came to the pageant to support me. As I've said, he really became a good friend and he remains a good friend to this day. Afterwards, Mom took us out to lunch.

TWENTY-TWO

Dad was having mood swings and suffering from depression. He became really introverted and went back to spending most of his time alone in his room. Friends stopped coming over on the weekends.

Mostly, he was quiet during this period of time. But he would still call me dummy now and then. If I started to say something, he would say, "Shut up. You don't know anything!"

Despite his depression, Dad had a good sense of humor. He could be very funny at times—but never with us kids. He was sometimes playful with Mom and liked to laugh and joke with others. He never shared that side of himself with me or my brothers. He would come around the corner silently and then just stand there. He was very intimidating and liked to make people jump.

Some years later, Dad would be diagnosed with bipolar disorder. I wasn't surprised. I had personally experienced all those years of him vacillating between depression and euphoria. I witnessed his obsessive behavior with hobbies, and his anger when he ripped the phone off the wall.

To make himself feel better, Dad started buying vehicles—lots of cars and a custom van. When I heard Mom and Dad yipping at each other over money, I figured Dad may have been depleting the budget by buying all these vehicles.

I could tell that beauty pageants were having a good effect on me. Regardless of whether or not I won, they did wonders for my self-confidence and self-esteem. And, it was nice to have Mom going shopping with me and cheering me on.

From the time I started doing beauty pageants, I always made sure my hair and makeup were done, and that made me look and feel better. I enjoyed the posing and practicing and learning to be a more graceful young lady. I was learning the ladylike way to get in and out of a car, for example.

It felt good to know I was becoming more of a lady—but I still knew I was tough. Welch women were tough, and I was a Welch woman. (Welch was my mom's maiden name.) Mom had always taught me that even if you weren't tough today, you could be tough tomorrow. She believed that whatever your troubles were today, tomorrow would always be better.

Thank God I had Mom, who was always picking me up and brushing me off. She always made me smile and gave me hope that tomorrow would be a better day. I was lucky to have her, especially considering that Dad was as verbally abusive as ever. He always told me that I didn't use the brain God gave me. Or, he'd say that if I had a brain, I'd be dangerous.

Words like that are damaging, and so were the physical beatings I sustained. That damage is with me to this day. I still recognize the effects of it within myself, just like I recognize it in a rescue dog that's been beaten or abused.

I was dating Mike, a nice young man who wasn't very tall. He lived down the street from us and was obsessed with the band, KISS. My parents had no problem with me dating. They trusted me to do the right thing. As I said, Dad was pretty much zoned out and stayed in his room anyway. So, he wasn't tuned in to my social life.

Mike and I only went out for a few weeks and then I moved on. He was very unhappy with our breakup—and he showed how upset he was by T.P.'ing our house. He also left on our front walkway a green, sculpted PlayDoh penis, about the size of a hand. I found it but I didn't know what I was looking at. So, I left it where it stood.

When Dad got up that afternoon, he was in the kitchen having his coffee. That's when he spotted the green penis through the kitchen window. He was angry and threw a fit—but I wasn't around to witness it. I was out somewhere at the time.

When I got home, Mom told me the whole story. Dad figured out that Mike, the boy who had TP'ed our house a few days earlier, was the same boy I had broken up with the week before. And, he figured that Mike had to be the culprit behind this prank. So, he picked up the green penis, sat it on the dash of the car, and drove to Mike's house.

Mom went along for the ride. She said that she knew how Dad was when he was angry. So, as they drove over there, she was afraid for Mike and his family.

When Dad arrived on the doorstep of Mike's family's home, he knocked on the door. When the dad answered the door, he found my dad holding the green PlayDoh penis straight up, by the balls.

"This belongs to you people," he said. "Keep your trash down on this side of the street!"

Dad shoved the penis into the chest of Mike's dad, who was no taller than five-foot-two.

"And keep your boy down here if you know what's good for you!" said Dad.

Mom was sitting in the car during this scene, and that's where she stayed. She said that Mike's dad's eyes were as big as saucers.

Years later, I saw Mike, and we sat down together over coffee. He told me that he had married a stripper, had a baby, and was living a happy life. It was clear that he wanted me to feel like I had missed out, big-time, by breaking up with him. He painted such a rosy picture of his life.

Neither one of us mentioned the stunt he had pulled, or what my dad did in response. I will say that I have always loved the Incredible Hulk. He was so big and strong and powerful, I didn't even mind that he was green.

As I went into eleventh grade, I had a busy life, between school and dating. I was notified that I was chosen to be Miss National Teen Clearwater again. I wasn't sure whether or not I wanted to go through with it again. I wondered if maybe no one else from my town had tried out.

I decided that I would accept being Miss National Teen Clearwater again. I said to myself, *I'll do it better this year.*

The only thing was, this time I was expected to write a 100-word essay to present in the talent portion of the pageant. The previous year, the talent portion was done as a group. I never did show Mom the essay I wrote. She asked me to but when I didn't, she didn't push me.

As you know by now, my parents had been very strict during my early life. By this point in time, they pretty much let me roam free. They didn't like it when I came home too late but other than that, they let me do my own thing. They took the same approach with my brothers. At the time, I liked having complete freedom. Looking back on it, I'm not sure it was the best thing for me.

Mom had bought me the most beautiful white chiffon dress for the pageant. It was the most expensive dress in the shop. Between the dress and the earrings and accessories she bought me to go with it, she paid $350.00. Mom loved shopping for me and loved to buy me things I wanted, like Jordache jeans.

My friend Debbie from junior high was also entered in the pageant as Miss National Teen Tarpon Springs. She represented her town and I represented mine. She lived down the road from me, but we didn't see each other much. It was nice to know that she was going to be in the pageant too. That made the entire experience all the more enjoyable.

I had asked sweet Mrs. Brunson, my favorite teacher from Clearwater High School, to help me with my pageant essay on the topic, *What's Right About America?*

At first, I was embarrassed to ask her to help me. I told her, "I have this pageant and I have to write an essay, but I don't want anyone to know that you helped me!"

The school wanted a picture of me so the yearbook committee could do a write-up about my pageant awards. The thing was, I had missed school picture day. So, the school called my house for an updated picture of me. Mom sent in a glamorous pageant photo.

I didn't realize what she'd done until the yearbook came out, right before I was leaving for the pageant. Between the write-up on me and the photo, it took up half a page. I went from being invisible in high school—the way I liked it—to being the center of attention.

At school, kids I didn't know were suddenly coming up to me. I didn't have a lot of friends and I wasn't used to that kind of attention. Instead of feeling proud of having the writeup and the pretty picture of me in the yearbook, all the attention made me really uncomfortable.

I spent the entire drive to the pageant rehearsing my speech. I was trying to memorize the words but no matter what I did, I couldn't memorize it. Thanks to my head injury as a child, I could say something five hundred times and still not remember it. I started to panic and get upset. I was already nervous as it was, and Dad was not helping the matter any. He kept teasing me.

When it was my turn to walk out onstage, I walked out in my evening gown with Dad as my escort. It made me feel good to have my dad with me, but it was nerve-wracking at the same time. With Dad, you never knew what to expect. He could knock you out flat if he thought you were looking at him sideways. This was only the second time Dad had ever attended one of my pageants.

When it was time to deliver my speech about America from my essay, I walked out in an outfit Mom had made specially for me. It was my red-white-and-blue fringe vest with a white satin skirt. Standing on the stage, I looked out at a sea of what looked like thousands of people, but I couldn't put my eyes on my parents. The lights were so bright, they were making me squint.

Between the lights and the enormous crowd, I completely forgot everything I had rehearsed in the car on the way there. I had seen some of the girls ahead of me walk onstage and completely forget what they were going to say. It made me really nervous to see them getting stage fright and panicking.

I smiled wide, slapped the side of my legs, and said, "Oh, I just forgot!"

Then I walked offstage. What else could I do? On the way off the stage, I passed by the judges' table and kept smiling. I felt confident and happy that I had made it through the pageant. I found joy in finishing things. I never felt the need to be perfect.

When we first arrived at the pageant, I took a seat at the table and talked to all seven of the judges. Each one of them asked me a question.

"What do you want to do when you grow up and move away from home?" asked one of the judges.

"Well, I'm interested in politics and I'd love to find a way to help a lot of people," I said.

The judge rolled her eyes like she was thinking, "Yeah, right! Good luck with that!"

I was totally taken aback by the judge's rude attitude toward me. I thought, *How snotty! Who crushes someone's dreams like that? I should've just said I wanted to be a hairdresser!*

There was a photographer at the pageant, taking pictures of all the girls. I had some of my modeling school photos with me and decided to see if I could get some tips from him.

I showed him the photos and asked him, "Do you think these poses are good? Are they age appropriate?"

He liked my photos and encouraged me to pursue modeling. So, I had the rude judge slap me in the face and push me down, and the nice photographer pick me up and encourage me. I had a lot of up-and-down emotions during that pageant.

All the girls got back into their evening gowns so the judges could pick the winner. There were about a hundred and fifty of us onstage. I was standing on the left side of the stage in the back, wondering where Debbie was standing. There were so many girls onstage, I couldn't see her. I was very uncomfortable standing there in that mob of girls with the bright lights on me.

The judges were calling out the names and titles of different girls, Miss This and Miss That. The next thing I knew, I heard them call my name. They gave me the title of Most Photogenic!

Oh, my God! I said to myself. *Me? Really?* I looked around in disbelief, sure I must be hearing things—just like you see women do in beauty pageants on T.V.

I made my way through the girls and ran up front to get my huge trophy. I was so proud of that. When I got back in line, holding my trophy, other girls were congratulating me and patting me on the back.

All of a sudden, my name was called a second time. Once again, I was in complete disbelief. I ran back up to the front of the stage. I won an $800 scholarship to the Barbizon Modeling School.

I thought, *I've won twice? Wow!*

I was so happy. I was just having a good time being Miss National Teen Clearwater in the pageant, wearing my beautiful new dress and fun red-white-and-blue outfit. And it was great having my mom and dad there. I never expected to win anything.

When I returned to school after the pageant, more people seemed to know me from my writeup and photo in the yearbook. Since people I didn't know were saying hi to me, it gave me a chance to make some more friends.

Being more popular had its ups and downs. There were different groups of kids at the school and they each hung out in a different spot. There were the jocks, and they hung out in the school parking lot. One day they picked up my little Spitfire and moved it to the other end of the parking lot. It was now sticking out in the driveway.

That was the first time I had ever been visible enough to be pranked before. I couldn't decide whether I was mad about the prank or happy. I had to admit that it was kind of cool to be popular enough to have kids messing with me.

TWENTY-THREE

IN MY SATURN Street neighborhood in Clearwater, I had a great group of friends. From time to time, everyone still drove down to the corner to hang out. I would jump into whichever car had a spot for me, or follow behind in my own little car.

As you might remember from earlier in the book, my friend Todd's dad owned a junkyard. My dad and Todd's dad had made some kind of a deal that led to bad blood between them. My dad felt that he had held up his end of the bargain and they were even—but Todd's dad didn't see it that way.

Despite the animosity between our parents, Todd and I stayed friends and we are friends to this day. Todd always had the best vehicles. One time, he picked up our entire group of friends in a van someone had dumped at the junkyard. He drove a ways down the road and then pulled off into a field of trees.

He started weaving in between the trees, going really fast. Every time he made a turn, we went flying around the back of the van, laughing our heads off. Then Todd took it a step further and started slamming the van into trees. When he hit a tree, all of us in the back of the van would shift to one side, laughing. Then Todd would restart the van, and slam into another tree so we all slid to the other side of the van.

Meanwhile, the dad of our friend Kent owned a lot of property. We would have bonfires on a piece of land he owned off U.S. 19. (As an interesting note, a plot of land he sold was used as the location for the first Hooter's Restaurant.)

One night, we were having a bonfire. Todd got into a conversation with a Canadian guy. He was new to our group of friends and must have tagged along with someone. Todd had driven to the bonfire in a Toyota junker, and the other guy had shown up in a monster truck.

"You ever run over anything with that truck?" Todd said.

"All the time!"

"Want to run over that little Toyota?"

The guy agreed that running over the Toyota sounded like fun. We were all surprised that it took three or four tries for the guy to flatten the Toyota. The boys appreciated the spectacle more than I did.

I had a good instinct for trouble. When I saw my friends getting a little too crazy, I would hightail it out of there. That's why I always made sure to have my own car—my escape vehicle!—with me whenever possible.

During spring break, I loved to go to concerts. We would gather a group of friends, pile into five cars and head to concerts at Dayton Beach or Disney World. One time, I dragged a bunch of my friends along to a Jan and Dean concert. I loved the adventure of being with my friends and away from home, and it didn't much matter what we were doing.

I became friends with Donna and Lynn, the sisters in the Perkins family from Boston. I was also friends with Bobby and Johnny, the two boys in the family. All four of the kids fit into our group of friends perfectly.

I thought their Boston accents were so cool. I could sit around, drinking beers with them, listening to them talk until the cows came home. We've carried our friendship all the way into the present day. Donna, the older sister, came and visited me recently. The younger sister, Lynn, had long straight hair that always made me think of Morticia from the T.V. show, *The Addams Family*.

One hot Saturday afternoon, I drove my little yellow convertible twenty minutes across town to the house my brother John shared with roommates. I was in the habit of walking into their house without knocking and that's what I did that afternoon. I looked around and noticed that they had a mess in the sink.

Oh, they must have partied last night, I said to myself. *I think I'll do their dishes for them and clean up their place a little bit.*

Before I started on the dishes, I needed a drink of something cold. I was hot and sweaty. So, I went over to the fridge, opened it, and saw a big frosty pitcher of something that looked to be iced tea. I was so thirsty, I took three or four huge gulps without even breathing.

The next thing I knew, Little Joe, one of John's roommates, came in. He slammed the pitcher out of my hand, causing it to crash to the floor.

I was shocked. "Did I drink your favorite drink or something?" I said. "Sorry about that!"

"You just drank mushroom tea!" he said. "*Magic* mushroom tea!"

Now that he mentioned it, I *had* noticed that the beverage tasted like dirt. I knew that John wasn't into drugs so I figured the mushroom tea must have belonged to one of his roommates.

I suddenly noticed that my throat felt weird—like it was filled with phlegm.

When Little Joe grabbed me by the arm and started pulling me out the door, I tried to pull away. I wasn't much for people coming at me. I'd had enough of that at home.

"What are you doing?" I said. "I just got here!"

"No, no, no . . . you've got to get home, fast! You're going to start coming onto the mushrooms and hallucinating pretty soon! Is your mom home? Can we call her to come get you?"

My mom was always the one to save everyone from everything. She was everyone's go-to person. Unfortunately, she didn't answer the phone. So, Little Joe put me in the car and drove straight to my house.

On the way home, I was wondering what was going to happen to me from drinking the tea. I was a little bit scared. Little Joe, on the other hand, was in a full-blown panic and really freaked out.

I couldn't understand why—but then I did.

When we got to the door, Mom was coming down the hall. She saw Little Joe dragging me by the arm. She asked what was up and Little Joe explained what had happened.

Little Joe gave Mom the scoop and then asked whether or not Dad was up. All my friends knew what Dad was like, and tried to stay clear of him as much as they could.

"What should I do for her?" asked Mom.

"Take her in her room and stay with her," said Little Joe.

John's friend Jimmy happened to be at my house at the time. (Mom had an open-door policy for the neighborhood kids.) Jimmy overheard what was being said.

"I don't have anywhere to go," he said. "I'll hang out with her." He thought I was kind of cute and didn't mind spending time with me.

I wasn't allowed to have boys in my room. So, we decided to go into Ricky's room. He was out at the time. Ricky had fighter-pilot wallpaper on his walls. For the next seven hours, I watched those planes fly up and off the wallpaper. I laughed, I cried, I tripped, and all the while, my stomach was in a wrench. (Psilocybin mushrooms are notorious for causing stomach distress.)

Jimmy was a great babysitter that day, very sweet and kind. When he saw me stumbling around the room all whacked out of my mind, he said, "Sit down or lay down, Suzette, or you're going to fall down!" He had me lay my head in his lap. Then he put a cold washcloth on my forehead.

Dad's room was right next to Ricky's. I phased in and out of concern that Dad would hear me laughing or crying. Thankfully, he kept his T.V. turned on 24/7 and that created background noise.

That experience with the mushroom juice reinforced my feeling that drugs were not for me. Other than taking an occasional hit off a joint, I'd never really been into drugs much in the first place. I mostly kept my partying limited to drinking.

I noticed that my mom was around much more often and seemed happier than usual. I also noticed that she lit up whenever my friend Todd's brother Paul was at our house. Mom seemed to pay extra attention to him, and they had long conversations.

I thought nothing of it. I had gone on a date with him once, but

I felt that he was too old for me. He was about ten years younger than my mom.

One day, I said to myself, *Wait a minute . . . Mom's actually flirting with this guy! And he's flirting back!*

I tried to ignore it and look the other way, but it went on for weeks. I started to get mad at my mom. *That's not very nice and not very moral!* I thought.

I was completely torn and didn't know how to feel or what to think. I had always wanted my mom to be treated kindly and with respect. And I knew that she could do better than Dad. Then again, I felt loyal to Dad, simply because he was my dad.

Mom and Paul started spending a lot of time together. While Dad was holed up in his bedroom, they would run out to the store together. Dad didn't see what was going on. Or maybe he was so down on life, he no longer cared.

He had spent the previous two years in his room. He had lost all his zest for life—not that he'd ever been a happy guy. The only enjoyment he ever seemed to get came from mocking, aggravating, and taunting people.

Now, it was like Dad wasn't even there. The morphine and Demerol had turned him into a shell of a man. He didn't seem to have any emotions anymore. He wasn't angry or sad or anything. He was just there, in his room. His life was now limited to eating and sleeping.

I knew that Mom and Paul were having an affair. I could see the sparkle in Mom's eye. So, it wasn't too surprising when she came to me and said, "What would you think if I left your father?"

I said to myself, *Mom's finally leaving that monster!*

I said, "Do what your heart makes you feel you need to do." I put the decision back in her lap.

The problem was, her heart really seemed to be with this young man, Paul. She was also tired of living with my dad, who was there physically but gone in his mind, soul and personality.

Even though part of me felt guilty for giving Mom the green light to leave Dad, I was really happy to see her happy. She was starting to dress better, look better and take better care of herself. She was selling real estate, part time, and also had a part-time job in an office downtown.

I was finally getting my mom back, and it felt great. I had been feeling like my brothers and I didn't even have parents anymore, between Mom partying with my friends and Dad spending all his time alone in his room, asleep.

TWENTY-FOUR

ON A SATURDAY morning in 1981 when I was seventeen years old and in my last year of high school, Mom came to each of us kids individually and made it official.

She said, "I'm leaving Richard . . ."

When she told us this, I remembered my words to her about following her heart. I felt like I had influenced her decision. In looking back, I think maybe I should have said, "Don't leave Dad. If you do, it will disrupt our whole family!"

Mom continued, saying, ". . . I don't know what I'm going to do. And, I don't know what he's going to do. All I know is that I'm leaving. I just wanted you to know."

I was happy for Mom and sad for Dad—but not that sad. I am not sure why I didn't feel worse for Dad. It must have been because of all the years of cruelty he put me through. He was mean and cruel to everyone, and all that cruelty came flooding back to me.

I knew that Mom was the glue that held him together. Now, he wouldn't have her anymore. Dad was always the strong one, the rock, and Mom was the sweet one. It seemed like everyone, including Dad, took advantage of Mom. But in their own way, they held each other up.

I didn't know how to measure their mutual support against all the terrible things Dad said and did to Mom. He laughed at her, berated her, and made fun of her. Dad had been tearing Mom down for years. Her affair with Paul had given her the spark she desperately needed to start to rebuild some self-confidence and self-esteem inside herself.

Dad tore me down in a similar way. He would tell me over and over again, "Only the strong survive, and you're weak. You're never going to survive!"

After being put down so many times, and told I was too weak to survive, I started to wonder, *Is Dad right? Am I too weak to survive?*

Mom didn't seem overly concerned with what would become of us kids after she was gone. Maybe that was because we were all running in our own directions by then anyway, and nobody was checking in with anybody else. We were all acting very independently of each other.

Ricky was still young but he was rarely home. He usually stayed at the home of his friend Casey, or other friends, and did his own thing. Everyone was okay with that. I was still going to beauty school. And John was working construction.

Mom said she was planning on moving to California, and Dad was planning on moving to Ohio. Mom didn't leave for California right away. Instead, she rented a two-bedroom apartment a few blocks from Dad. She was trying to make it easy for us kids to go back and forth between the two households until she left. The truth was, she got it mostly for me, John, and Ricky.

The only thing was, it drove Dad nuts to have Mom so nearby but be unable to be with her. He started calling her and bothering her. He would see her car out in front of the new place, and call to tell her he knew that she was home. That was Dad—he had stalker tendencies.

Mom quickly realized that she wasn't far enough away from Dad. She was gone but not really gone. So, she came to us kids and told us that the time had come for her to move to California. She said that Angel was going to drive out there with her.

Dad was not living in our family home anymore. He was now living in an apartment across town from the one Mom rented for us. Before Mom said she was leaving Dad, I had found a little house for myself to move into, but I gave that up. I was still spending some nights in our family house, and so were my brothers. So, we had the apartment Mom rented for us, the family house, and Dad's apartment in Largo. John, Ricky and I were running back and forth between our three places.

Dad had decorated his apartment with beautiful new furniture. But when Mom took off and went to California, Dad got mad and left for Ohio—just to prove a point.

In the meantime, our white German Shepard, Jake, ran into a garbage truck and got hit. Now he had pins in his leg, so we had to carry him around. We took him over to Dad's apartment where Ricky was now staying, and he kept an eye on Jake.

Each of us reacted differently to the split. Ricky didn't seem to have much of an emotional reaction to Mom and Dad's breakup. He was his usual quiet self. The only time I saw him show any emotion over it was when he cried after having a drink one day. He wasn't in the habit of drinking at such a young age. So, I attributed his show of emotion to the fact that he'd been drinking.

Mom had left behind her custom van when she took off for California. Dad continued driving his Cadillac. I still had my Spitfire. John, Ricky and I now had three places to live, three cars, and plenty of money at our disposal. So, it was no surprise that we were suddenly very popular.

We were running wild, spending, cruising and living the dream. I hardly noticed that we were alone without any parents. Not that they'd been very involved in our lives, even before they left the state. I had been running around on my own for a while by that time.

Once the house sold, Dad started moving everything out. I moved a lot of it out, myself. We didn't even bother cleaning the house. It was while moving things out that it really hit me: this was going to be a real change.

Mom came back from California and Dad came back from Ohio—with a girlfriend. She was quiet with dark hair.

"Do you need a car?" Dad asked.

I thought, *Why not?* I said, "Sure, I need a car."

"Well, take her car," said Dad. He gave me her little Dodge.

I thought, *Why would he want to leave her without a car?*

The truth was, Dad wanted to take away the woman's independence. If she couldn't take her own car and go anywhere, Dad would have control over her.

I took the woman's car and drove it for a while. It was fun to be driving a different car. Eventually, I returned it to Dad.

It became obvious that, new girlfriend or not, Dad was the same person. He hadn't changed. He started drinking a lot and ended up losing his girlfriend.

Once Dad was alone again, all hell broke loose. He started harassing Mom and picking fights with people.

One night, Dad, my brother John, and their friends were hanging out at the Banana Boat Bar, having drinks.

They ended up getting into a fight with someone over a pool game. Someone suggested they take the fight outside. Dad's Cadillac was parked by the door of the bar. He opened the trunk, knowing his golf clubs were in there, and started tossing them to my brother John and everyone on their side of the fight.

The next time I saw Dad, he told me this story, laughing.

Instead of thinking the story was funny, I just thought Dad was drinking too much. Knowing that Dad no longer had Mom's calming influence in his life, I was a little bit worried.

John rented an apartment in a big complex. "Why don't you come over here and rent a place by me?" he suggested.

So, I called my friend Lou from high school (not Tattoo Lou) and said, "Hey, do you want to be my roommate?"

I knew that Lou always had a good job and would be reliable and pay the rent on time. He agreed, and we rented an apartment above John's. Then Ricky joined us too. He ran up and down the stairs between our two places. It felt really good to know where Ricky was, and know that he was okay. As I've said, his quiet, introverted ways had been worrying me and making me wonder how he would do out on his own. I always felt protective over him.

One night while I was sleeping, I heard a loud pounding on my door. When I opened it, Dad was standing there with his arm raised. In his hand was a knife. I could smell liquor on his breath. He started screaming at me, saying that my student loan was being repaid from his Social Security check.

I knew that wasn't true. I had just recently taken out the loan. There

was no way they would be coming after Dad for that money so soon—
or ever for that matter. I also knew that when Dad was in one of his dark
moods, facts didn't matter. He was drunk and making up something to
fight about.

I ducked under his arm and ran barefoot down the stairs. I was
going so fast, I got blisters on my feet. I hopped into my car and turned
the key. Thank goodness my mom had taught me to leave the key in the
car. That way, I could always make a quick getaway.

Dad turned around and started chasing me down the stairs. Running
down the stairs after me, he tripped and fell down the last two or three
stairs.

As I drove away in my car, I saw Dad getting up. I was scared, my
feet were blistered, and my heart was beating out of my chest.

I knew there was only one way he could have known where I lived:
either Ricky or John had told him.

Oh, my God! I said to myself. *Now Dad knows where I live! I can't
live here anymore.*

I started selling some of my belongings in preparation for the move.
I had also bought a washing machine for the new place from Ricky for
$75.00. When I went to pick it up, there were two other people there to
pick it up, as well. I was so mad at Ricky, who had apparently sold it out
from under me. At the same time, there was a silver lining.

I said to myself, *It looks like Ricky's got some hustle in him after all!
Maybe he's more of a survivor than I thought. He shouldn't hustle his
sister, but still . . . it's a good sign.*

I rented a little two-bedroom house off Cleveland Street in
Clearwater, on a corner by a hotdog shop. John had also given up his
apartment, so he and Ricky came and stayed with me too. We were
living there month to month. We couldn't afford the rent, or much of
anything else, for that matter.

When Mom got back into town, she got a job at a real estate company.
Her office was right off Cleveland Street. Her relationship with Paul was
very short-lived and had now ended. It served its purpose, reminding

Mom that she was still beautiful and men still found her attractive. It was a wakeup call.

Mom was looking pretty again, with her blonde hair and slimmer figure. She had gotten her smile back. Most importantly, she had gotten herself out from under Dad's tyranny. She had freed us kids from it at the same time.

John was still doing roofing and construction work. He moved into his own apartment on U.S. Highway 19 in Clearwater—a big road that runs all the way through town. Next to his unit lived a guy from Iran and his brother.

The guy's name was Sharif. He was tall and thin and claimed to be a prince. Sharif liked me and started following me around, offering to take me here and there. After we hung out a little bit, he asked me to become one of his wives. I guess he was planning on having a harem.

I called my mom, saying, "Mom! I'm so excited! Sharif asked me to be one of his wives!"

"What are you talking about, Suzette? If you go with him back to Iran, he could have seven other wives. You don't know how many there will be. Not only that but he could kill you if he doesn't like the way you act!"

I hadn't considered the fact that our relationship in America, with him taking me nice places and us having fun together, would change back in Iran. The turning point came one day while we were driving down U.S. Highway 19. We passed some firemen standing on the corner at the light, and they were collecting money for a children's home.

I love to give, so I was digging in my purse for change. I found some change to give the guy. I saw that Sharif also had a quarter on the dash. When I went to grab his quarter, he smacked my hand away and rolled up his car window. My money fell out of my hand.

"You do not give a beggar money!" he shouted.

It was very scary. It shocked me back to my senses. I thought, *Whoa! Mom's right! Sharif can be nice one minute but ordering me around the next! In his country, women are not respected. Iran's no place for this American woman.*

Around this time, I got diagnosed with sleep apnea. I'd been having symptoms for a while. I got a CPAP machine and was finally able to get a good night's sleep. I felt like a new person.

I got a job at a hotdog shop and went to work for a little Greek man. He was always yelling at us employees in Greek. One thing that drove him nuts was the braids in my hair.

The black girls at the beauty academy where I was studying had done my braids for me. I was learning how to style black-girl hair and they were learning how to style white-girl hair.

I had told these girls about having to wear my hair off my face at work. So, they came up with the idea to braid my hair like Bo Derek in the popular movie *10*.

"We did it! We got your hair off your face!" they said, very proud of themselves.

I looked in the mirror and I was horrified. But I didn't have the heart to ask the girls to remove the braids. It had taken several of them to put all the braids in my hair and I knew how hard they had worked on it. They had even put beads in the braids.

My boss yanked out one of the beads in my hair and shouted, "NO!"

I thought, *Oh, my God! What does he want me to do?*

He grabbed a red bandana and started shaking it at me. This was his way of letting me know that he expected me to put that over my hair. He let me work for two hours with the bandana covering my braids, and then he said, "You go home! You come back, no hair braids!"

Now *that* I understood. I didn't work there long before realizing I needed to move on.

I was happy knowing that Mom was back in town and both my brothers were around. Since Mom was busy with her real estate activities, I offered to cook Thanksgiving dinner for everyone. I had never cooked a turkey before. Mom was guiding me as to what to do. The only thing was, she wasn't around the entire time. She was in and out of the house, along with both of my brothers.

I had to run to a nearby store to pick something up for Thanksgiving dinner. When I got back, there was a shopping cart in front of the house. I thought that was odd but I didn't think much of it.

When I got inside my house, I found a grubby, greasy old man sitting at the dining room table. I had an open-door policy at the house, and people came and went. Usually the people who came and went were people we knew, and they were around our age.

"Howdy, Ma'am!" said the old man.

I was irritated to find this man was in my house. I gave him a fake smile and said, "Who are you here with?"

"That cowboy there," he said.

My brother John had been bringing stray dogs, cats and people in off the street all our lives. He was trying to do something beautiful and sweet by including this man in our Thanksgiving dinner.

I just felt bitchy and irritated, seeing this grubby man at our dinner table. I snapped out of it and told John, "Absolutely, let him stay!"

I told myself, *It's no big deal. It will be kind of fun having him here! We can tell stories and enjoy having company.*

The poor man never touched the silverware, preferring to use his filthy hands to eat. I don't know how he chewed his food. There wasn't a tooth in his head. While he ate, I washed his clothes for him.

That was the way our family operated. We would open up our hearts to others. I would have been miserable married to a man who slapped a quarter out of my hand as I tried to give it to charity.

Ever since his divorce from Mom, Dad had really been hitting the bottle hard. One night, he was driving drunk and caused a terrible accident. He was totally out of it and failed to stop at a stoplight. He slammed into the back of a lady's car. Since he hadn't even slowed down, he was going forty to fifty miles per hour at the time. The poor woman was paralyzed for life.

Dad was arrested for DWI, due to the mixture of medication and alcohol in his system. He was also sued by the woman he hit. He was living on his disability check and didn't have any assets or money. Or, nothing anyone could see in a bank account, anyway.

I was so mad at Dad for driving while intoxicated and ruining that lady's life. He was on a terrible downward spiral. Then he got a new girlfriend named Cathy who owned a bar. Maybe she reminded him of the days when he and Mom owned the bar in Minnesota. Dad started working at Cathy's bar. He also did some renovations around her house. They started fighting and Cathy kicked Dad out.

Dad did not take kindly to being kicked out of her house. He found a way back inside and took an axe to the place. He axed the ceiling fan he helped install, the bed he helped put together, and the bathroom he was renovating. He set out to destroy every spot in the house where he had put in his sweat labor. By the time the police got to the house to stop Dad, he had axed up Cathy's entire house. He went crazy.

Dad never did have to pay for his crime. Cathy may have been too scared of him to press charges. That was Dad's way. Any time he was in trouble with the law, he would find the best lawyer he could. Somehow the lawyers always got Dad off. I do know that back in those days, the police did not necessarily jail people for domestic disputes.

When I heard about this incident, I was even angrier at Dad—and I stayed mad. Even though he wasn't physically abusing *me* at the time, I was mad at him for hurting others.

TWENTY-FIVE

ONCE AGAIN, MOM, John, Ricky and I had all scattered and were living our own lives. Since I was on my own again, I needed a room to rent in order to continue attending Le Boutique Beauty Academy—my new, fancy beauty school.

So, I moved in with Rick, a friend of a friend. He lived in Ozona, Florida, about ten miles from Clearwater. The town was a bit more rural than Clearwater, and our bungalow reminded me of a cabin. We had neighbors but they weren't close. The place had a huge screened-in porch. Being out on the porch reminded me of going camping.

Rick was the perfect roommate—and then we started dating. Rick was a twenty-eight-year-old engineer. Being with an older, stable guy really appealed to me. I liked knowing what was going to happen every day and having some kind of predictability in my life. We loved watching the T.V. show *Dynasty* together and doing other homey things.

We had just started dating when we moved in together, and suddenly we were playing house and living like a married couple.

One night right before I'd moved in with Rick, I was driving Mom's car and hit a telephone pole. I had been partying at Studio 19, a nightclub. When I left the club, I fell asleep at the wheel. I was exhausted all the time, between attending beauty school and working nights as an instructor at a fitness center.

I blacked out in the wreck. When I came to, I lifted my head and saw a man standing at the driver's side of my car, with a cigarette dangling from his mouth. He was talking to me out of the side of his mouth.

I rolled down my window in time to hear him say, "Hey, missy, are you alright?"

I could smell alcohol on the guy's breath. "I'm going to be alright," I said, "but is there any way you could pull the pole off my car so I can leave?"

He surveyed the situation and said, "You're kind of stuck." Even though he was drunk, he would have probably pulled the pole off my car if he'd been able to.

"You'd better get the hell out of here!" he said. "The cops are probably coming."

The police gave me a ticket for driving without insurance because I couldn't find my mom's insurance card. I had no idea whether Mom even had insurance, or the name of her carrier if she did. (We always drove each other's cars in my family, and I happened to be driving Mom's car at the time of the accident.)

I got stuck with a $1,400 bill for the telephone pole. That was the end of my mom's car. She had been out of town at the time of the accident. When she got back and found out about the wreck, she wasn't happy about it, but she was glad I was okay.

Mom said she was done with the car anyway. She hadn't made a payment on the car in a couple of months and the car company was looking to repossess it. So, I called the car company and told them where they could pick up the car.

Out of the blue, I got a call from Daddy John. I was shocked. As I've said, my brother John went back and forth between our house and Daddy John's. But I hadn't even heard Daddy John's voice since I was a little girl.

"I would like to see you," he said. "I'll buy you a ticket if you'd like to come see us. I'd also like to give you a final child-support payment so then I can be done with it."

He was about done with child-support payments and wanted to give me a lump sum to finish off his obligation. The law was that if your child was attending college, you had to continue paying child support until they were twenty-one. Otherwise, the payments stopped when the child turned eighteen. He was planning to give me the lump sum to go toward my beauty school. He also seemed to genuinely want to see me.

I didn't care about the money. I was just excited that Daddy John was finally showing some interest in me. As I boarded the plane, I was still in a state of shock. I was actually on my way to see my birth father after so many years. When I landed in Toledo, Ohio, Daddy John was there, waiting to pick me up. I recognized his face from photos.

Wow, I said to myself, *he looks so much like John!* Daddy John was good looking like my brother John, and they both had the same fair, Polish skin.

When Daddy John hugged me tightly, I was uncomfortable and a little bit pissed. I wanted to say, *Oh, really? You're so happy to see me? Well, where were you when I was getting beaten? Things were bad in my house! If you really cared about me, you wouldn't have let me go through everything I had to go through.*

I didn't let him know what I was feeling. I smiled and was pleasant to him as we walked to his car. When Daddy John started driving me to Grandma Lottie's house, I was confused. I was very familiar with Grandma's house, but I had never in my entire life been to Daddy John's house. I had really been looking forward to seeing it.

There was so much I wanted to know about Daddy John and his life. When I was lying in bed after a beating from Dad, I'd wonder about Daddy John. I'd wonder how tall he was, how he smelled, and how he had changed since I last saw him.

I'd think to myself, *If he only knew how I was being treated, he'd come get me and love me and treat me right!*

Even though I was disappointed to be staying at Grandma's, I was happy to see her. (She was Daddy John's mom.) I loved her and she was the sweetest lady. She spoke very broken English. So, it was hard to understand what she was saying. But she was warm and wonderful, and I could feel the love in her voice whenever she talked to me. She had sent me a birthday card with ten dollars in it every birthday without missing one. I figured Daddy John owed me some cards.

In addition to being a sweetheart, Grandma was tough and a bit kooky. She would dance around the house and, in the middle of dancing, take her wig off and shake it.

While I was staying at Grandma's, I met my biological half-sister, Brenda. She said, "Dad says you and I look nothing alike, so we can't be sisters."

Apparently, my lack of resemblance to Brenda was all the proof Daddy John needed that I wasn't his daughter. Hearing that made me feel like Daddy John and I had taken two steps forward and one step back. I was bonding with him on this visit, but now he seemed to be back in denial mode about me being his daughter.

While I was at Grandma's house, she decided to perm my hair, using tiny little yellow rollers. While the perm was processing, I went next door to see the neighbor girl. While we were smoking a joint and drinking wine together, the time lapsed on my perm chemicals. I finally remembered that I needed to get back to Grandma's house so she could rinse out my hair.

"Oh, you've been gone a long time!" said Grandma in her broken Polish-English.

She removed the perming rollers and gave my hair a good rinsing.

I looked in the mirror and saw a white ball of fuzz on my head. I looked like a Q-Tip.

It was so cute of Grandma to perm my hair and I tried to be grateful. But it wasn't easy with this head of white fuzz. Of course, it was my fault for staying next door too long.

The same night I got my perm, Daddy John came over to Grandma's and said, "Come on, Suzette. Let's go out and party!"

Despite my Q-tip hairstyle, I went ahead and went out with Daddy John. He took me to a bar where a band was playing—and then, once we got inside, I saw very little of him. I had a couple of drinks, which is all I ever needed to get a buzz.

After a while, Daddy John came and got me. He said, "I'm going to my friend's house to party. Let's go."

I said to myself, *Wow, Dad parties more than my friends do!*

When I woke up the next morning at his friend's house, I realized that Daddy John had never gone home.

I was used to falling asleep on the couches of friends and didn't think it was any big deal. But I wasn't married with kids, like Daddy John. I figured he had everyone at his house worried. He had a wife he had married right after he left Mom, and they had a pack of kids.

He didn't seem at all concerned about getting home. I realized this probably wasn't the first time he had stayed out all night. Grandma later told me that he was naughty and mischievous, pulled every stunt there was to pull, and was boastful about it.

Daddy John dropped me off at Grandma's house and didn't even bother to come in. Grandma was mad that he had kept me out all night. She started yelling at me and cursing at Daddy John in Polish.

I felt sick from drinking the night before, and tried to revive myself in the shower. Then, I walked to the store with Grandma so I could buy the fixins to cook spaghetti for her. It was a nice day outside and I would have enjoyed the walk if not for being green under the gills.

The next day, I decided that while I was in town, I wanted to see my other grandma too. I hadn't seen Grandma Betty (Dad's mom) in ages and I missed her. So, I took a cab over to her house.

I loved Grandma Betty, but I also knew that she was a longtime alcoholic. So, I wasn't too surprised when she said, "Come on, Suzette. Let's go to a bar!"

I thought, *Oh, no . . . really? To a bar? I don't know if I can take any more alcohol!*

When Grandpa Red left for work around six o'clock, we caught a cab to the nearest bar. As soon as we took a seat at the bar, Grandma ordered one of those drinks where you drop a shot into a beer and down it all at once. Grandma and I started slamming these drinks and got totally trashed. Somehow, we made our way into a taxi and got back to her house.

The rest of the night, Grandma and I hid out from Grandpa Red. He came home from work in the middle of the night. I was sick in her bathroom in the back end of the house. I figured I was safe back there, since Grandpa stayed upstairs asleep once he got home from work.

I did fall asleep for a little while. When I awoke, I decided to take a look around. I was looking for family photos. There were no pictures of me or my family in there. But I did find a cabinet full of photos of neighborhood kids my grandmother treated like her own grandkids. I was so jealous.

I said, "Who are all these kids?"

"They're the neighbor kids," said Grandma.

I was thinking, *And while we're at it, why haven't you ever sent me a card or letter?*

I was hurt that pictures of us weren't in Grandma's house, but I didn't hold it against her. I felt like it was my mom's responsibility to send her family photos.

I was on day two of a terrible hangover when Daddy John came to pick me up at Grandma's house. I was still analyzing everything he did. I was looking for the ways in which we were and were not similar. He talked a mile a minute about being president of the union for his textile leather factory. He had worked there for thirty years, from the time I was a baby. A lot of people counted on him.

I was thinking, *Oh, my gosh! Will he ever take a breath? I can't get a word in edgewise!*

Then it hit me that I too am a fast talker. And I heard Mom's voice in my head, saying, "You're your father's daughter!"

That got me to thinking about all the things I had done and said during my lifetime that reminded me of Daddy John. Suddenly, I saw all those times he'd said I wasn't his differently.

I said to myself, *I know Daddy John is my dad! I don't need a DNA test to prove it. I'll bet he's just resentful over having to pay child support for me. Mom conceived me with him, and then left him while she was pregnant with me.*

He never did bring me over to see his house. But he did bring my half-sister, Holly, over to Grandma's to meet me. She was mentally handicapped. That was the first time I had ever met anyone who was handicapped. I didn't know how to talk to her.

As I left, Daddy John gave me three thousand dollars to put toward school expenses. He made it clear that he now considered us square in terms of his child-support payments.

I was disappointed that during our visit, Daddy John never once acknowledged that I was his daughter. I later realized that was never going to happen—just as Dad (Richard) was never going to say he was sorry for all the awful things he had done to me.

TWENTY-SIX

WHEN I GOT back to Florida, Rick and I started bickering and butting heads a little bit. That wasn't surprising, considering that he was Italian, and I have an Irish temper. That got me thinking about how we had been living together as a couple after dating for only a short period of time. The reality started to scare me. Things were moving too fast between us.

I decided it was time for me to leave Rick's house. So, I used the little bit of money I had to rent a place with Mom and my brothers. It was a nice, new, three-or-four-bedroom house in Palm Harbor.

Our dog Mutley had been with me my whole life, and I brought him with me to the new house. Mutley had seen better days and was getting on in years but I never thought of him as old. Then one day, he got out of the house while one of us was going in or out and wandered off somewhere. I never saw him again. I told myself that someone had found him and given him a new home. I couldn't bear to think that Mutley had wandered off somewhere to die.

While we were living in this house, Dad made it his mission to aggravate Mom. He kept coming around the house and pestering her. And when he wasn't there, he was calling to taunt and tease her. He may have been trying to win her back. If so, he had a totally backwards way of going about it. He did not win any points with my mother.

I had won a pageant the year before. Part of my prize winnings was a Miss Cover Girl photo shoot. The only problem was, in order to do the photo shoot, I needed to get a flight to New York City. By the time this opportunity came up, I'd already spent the money Daddy John had given me on beauty school expenses and a car.

I can't remember whether I asked Dad directly for help or Mom intervened for me. In any case, Dad refused to help me with the expenses for the trip. If I wanted to do the shoot, I was going to have to pay for my own plane ticket, food and spending money.

My feeling was that Mom was paying for everything for me. The least Dad could have done was help me cover expenses on my New York trip.

I thought, *He's just drinking all his money away!*

The more I thought about it, the madder I got. One day, I lost my temper and called Dad a bastard. I wasn't much for standing up to my dad, and it was almost unheard of for me to cuss him out.

I was also mad at Dad for wrecking my cute little Spitfire. He took it out one day when he had taken Quaaludes and had a few drinks, and that was the end of that car.

I found a job as a bartender at a neighborhood bar owned by Mom's friend, Angel. It was located by the beach in a rough part of town. Angel didn't seem to mind the neighborhood. She lived three doors down from her bar.

All the old drunks went to Angel's Bar. The problem was, I was never great at counting change and it slowed me down. One night, I was having a hard time keeping up with drink orders while a really drunk man was anxious for me to refill his beer pitcher.

He finally got fed up and hurled the pitcher at me from across the bar. I ducked and the pitcher hit the glass beer cooler behind me, shattering instantly.

Oh, my God! I said to myself. *This place is way too rowdy for me!*

I called Mom and told her what had happened. Then, Mom called Angel and told her that she needed to get someone in to replace me pretty quickly.

One day, Mom was at the Horseshoe Bar with a guy she had been dating. The ex-girlfriend of Mom's current boyfriend started talking smack about my mom.

I walked by just in time to hear this woman say something bad about my mom and call her a name. I grabbed the smack-talker by the back of her hair, pulled her off her barstool, and put my cigarette out in her face. I went from zero to violent in sixty seconds, just like my brother John. It was terrible. We were little powder kegs, and we could explode at any time, in any place.

The way I saw it, I was just protecting my mom. She was the sweetest, kindest person. She had never been in a fight in her entire life. I wasn't about to let some trashy girl give her trouble. I decided to eliminate the problem right then and there. And I did it cold sober.

I heard someone call across the bar, "That's Richard's daughter! Get her out of here before the cops come!"

Dad had been going to that bar for many years to gamble on pool and sports. He must have made a few friends. They were trying to get me out of there before I got in trouble with the police. Someone got me out of the bar and threw me in my car. I quit going to that bar for a while.

When Mom first started dating again after her divorce from Dad, she was dating all kinds of guys, from bikers to businessmen to a guy in a 1950s band.

So, I said to her, "You know how you always told me it's just as easy to marry a rich guy as a poor guy? Why aren't you listening to your own advice?"

"Well, Suzette, the heart wants what the heart wants."

Mom did date a businessman for a little while. When she mentioned that we needed a couch for our new place, he spent thousands on furniture for us.

"Mom, this guy's rich!" I said. "Why don't you settle down with him?"

She wasn't ready to settle down—or at least not with him. She had never had the chance to date. She had been in relationships with Fred, John and Richard. Now, she finally had a chance to take her time and choose a man she really wanted. She would finally find that man in a horse jockey named J.R.

Mom and J.R. met at Angel's bar. He only stood about five-foot-five. Mom was only five-foot-two. He was a tiny bit taller in his cowboy boots. One night when they hadn't been dating very long, Mom brought J.R. home so I could give him a haircut.

I jumped at the chance because I really needed practice cutting hair. I said to myself, *I could really get good at this is if I keep getting to cut everyone's hair!*

I had been drinking that night and shouldn't have been anywhere near a pair of scissors. And J.R. was downright drunk.

Perfect! I said to myself. *He's had a few so he'll be patient and nice to me.*

I gave J.R. the worst haircut ever, but I wasn't too worried about it. I told myself that I would never see him again. I was surprised to find him still there the following morning.

I had a fascination with the Sunshine Skyway Bridge over Tampa Bay, which had been recently rebuilt. Something about it spoke to me. It was a long concrete bridge which seemed to be suspended by wires which were actually cables. I thought this bridge was really beautiful.

I loved to drive really fast over the bridge, yelling and screaming as the wind hit my face. Sometimes Al would go with me. As we drove along, we forgot all our troubles. We kept the conversation light and enjoyed each other's company and the thrill of the drive. He was always my soft place to land. Al knew how happy it made me to drive fast over the bridge.

I had been partying one night on Quaaludes and gin-and-tonics. Around two or three in the morning, high as a kite, I decided to take a drive. I drove to the top of the bridge, put the car in park, and got out. I walked over to the edge. It was the first time I had ever gotten out of the car on the bridge. I used to go cliff jumping over the Rainbow River, so I wasn't afraid to lean over the side of the bridge.

The wind was blowing, and my hair was slapping my face. I tucked my hair behind my ears. Then I noticed a ladder and decided to climb down. I got three or four steps down the ladder and looked down. Big whitecaps were slamming against the concrete pylons holding up the bridge. It was a scary sight.

As the wind kept whipping my hair into my face and eyes, my face started to sting. I was struggling to see. Suddenly, I realized I was down five steps—further down than I meant to go—and I started to panic. Being drugged and drunk, I was in sort of a trance. I felt the waves and heard the sound they were making. I realized I was starting to get wet.

My hands felt slippery on the ladder. I realized that all I would have to do was let go of the ladder. I had seen T.V. shows where someone goes to a bridge to kill themselves and someone on the bridge stops them. But there had been no one there when I got out of the car. Nobody was there to try to save me. No one even stopped to question why a car was stopped on the bridge so late at night—a car that was left running with the keys still in it.

There was a little part of me that was suicidal. A couple of girls who had joined our group of friends had been bullying me. One of them punched me in the face. She roped my other friends into being mean to me too. My friends had become my family now that my parents were split up. Having my friends bully and abuse me like my dad used to do really hurt.

I already suffered from low self-esteem, and I was having a really hard time. I was questioning myself, wondering whether I was weak and might not survive like Dad had often told me.

I snapped out of it. I climbed up over the top of bridge, and saw that my car was still sitting there, running. I was so relieved. I ran and jumped into my car and drove away. It was a cold awakening of my soul. It sobered me up and made me realize what I almost did. I knew I needed to get more stable.

I'd had plenty of excitement and drama in my life, but stability had always been just out of my reach. As I got older, I began to look for stability and security—not only in a man but in my friends. I was starting to understand what that looked like, as I saw it in some of our neighbors.

I was hoping for Mom's sake that J.R. was stable. Even though I'd given him that horrible drunk haircut, probably the worst haircut of his life, he'd kept dating Mom. He turned out to be more of the gypsy type than the stable type. At least he was devoted to my mom. I think Mom may have always secretly had that gypsy spirit too.

We had all been talking about hustling up some money so we could buy Ricky a car, now that he was sixteen. We talked about each pawning some of our belongings or doing whatever we had to do to scare up the money for the car.

One day, Mom announced, "Dad won't leave me alone and I've got to get out of here. So, I'm going to go on the road with J.R. I'll just give Ricky my car." As a horse jockey, J.R. was always on the road, traveling on the racetrack circuit. And his trainer had a car they could use.

I was happy for Mom to get the chance to travel. She had spent so many years living like a prisoner in the house with Dad, who spent most of his time holed up in his room. It was like Mom was finally breaking out of her cell. Even after the divorce was final, she hadn't really been free because Dad wouldn't let go of her.

TWENTY-SEVEN

WHEN MOM LEFT to go on the road with J.R., that left me, Ricky and John living together in a little house. I felt responsible for Ricky, even though I was older by only a couple of years. I had always looked out for my little brother like a mother hen.

In the period before Mom took off with J.R., Ricky had been living his own life. So, it wasn't surprising that he wanted no part of me now trying to guide him. He wouldn't listen to me. I couldn't control him. When he took apart a motorcycle in the living room, that was the last straw for me. I was so mad, I told him to get out.

When Ricky refused to leave, I had the police come. "I am going to beauty school," I explained, "and I can't get my little brother to listen to me. Can you just get him out for me?"

"No," they said, "It's his house too. You can't just kick him out."

"Well, I'm paying for the house! He's supposed to be listening to me."

The officers told me, "We're sorry. We can't help you get him out."

Even though the police officers wouldn't help me kick Ricky out of the house, they did try to mediate between us.

They told him, "Look, you need to be respectful. Take that motorcycle outside to the carport area."

"What about this dog?" I said to the police officers. "I can't take care of her either!" Someone had dropped off a big dog, Georgette, at the house. I didn't know what to do with her. The police officer came back a few days later and adopted the dog.

After the visit from the police, Ricky got scared. He started to make himself scarce. He would get in his car and take off when he didn't like something I was saying or doing. He would wait for me to leave and then go back to the house. We were always passing each other.

Meanwhile, my brother John was restless and unsettled. He is protective and sentimental by nature and worries about everyone. He doesn't like change, probably as a result of having been shuffled around between our house and Daddy John's when he was young. John didn't know J.R. very well and didn't like the fact that Mom had married him so quickly.

Mom had come home one day after she'd been seeing J.R. for about a month and said, "He asked me to marry him!"

The wedding was held in a little nondenominational church about a block from our house. We all walked there.

For her wedding dress, Mom found a little pale blue V-neck dress at a secondhand store. It looked like a prom dress.

I wore one of my pageant dresses. It was lavender and white, with a high neck. Both of my brothers were dressed up. J.R. was wearing a tuxedo and he looked sharp—all hundred pounds of him.

The ceremony was really sweet. It seemed to fly by. Mom and J.R. exchanged vows, we took some photos, and then they were out of there. They got in their car, which was already packed, and drove to Oklahoma. Mom was the happiest I had ever seen her.

I thought to myself, *Well, Mom knew a man a month and just married him!*

I could tell that the situation was wearing on my brother John. At the same time, I was just a teenager, and I had simpler things on my mind, like the fact that John was always leaving his mess in the kitchen. I got pissed off and started calling him names. He reacted by ripping the cupboards off the wall. When he pulled the cupboards off the wall, he threw them off to the side. Then he shot out the door.

He's such a beast! I thought to myself.

I had been digging at John and getting his goat. I really got him upset. I knew what I was doing was wrong, but I thought nothing of it. My brother knew I loved him and I knew he loved me.

John stayed gone after that. Now, Mom was gone, and John was gone. That left just Ricky and me at the house.

Now that Mom was out of town with J.R., I started relying a bit on Bobby. He was the brother of my friend Donna. They had lived down the street from us on Saturn Street. I'd never paid much attention to Bobby and his blue eyes and dark curly hair. Everyone was drawn to him, but I wasn't impressed. I saw him as a player. I wanted nothing to do with him and his ways—romantically, anyway.

Bobby and I were sharing a place together. My old friend Lou was our third roommate. Over time, Bobby started to wear me down. He was so charming. I would be talking and out of the blue, he would say, "You are so beautiful!"

"No, *you* are so beautiful!" I would say back to him. It was funny.

While I was attending beauty school, I met my friend Julie. She had long red hair and one of those laughs you could hear in the next room. I was really drawn to her and loved her from the minute I saw her smile. She was studious, well-spoken, together and calm.

She and I were so different, I don't know how we even became friends. To this day, we are close friends.

The first night we hung out together, she wanted to stop by her boyfriend's house to say hello. While Julie went into the house, I waited in the car. After a while, I got tired of sitting there. I started blinking the lights and honking the horn. Finally, I couldn't take it anymore. I got out of the car and went inside the house.

As Julie let me in, she said, "Hang on . . . Rodney's getting himself together." We were all going to have drinks at Ollie's, a neighborhood tavern.

Suddenly, there was a violent pounding on the door. Someone was yelling for us to open the door. When we did, policemen were standing there with their weapons drawn. They ordered us to drop to the floor.

The Clearwater Police burst in, filling the house. They already had it surrounded outside. I was obviously caught in the middle of a major bust. Rodney was handcuffed, brought outside along with his brother, and put in the back of a police car.

Julie and I were put in handcuffs, read our Miranda rights, and put into the back of a separate police car.

All of this drama was courtesy of Rotten Rodney. From the day I met him, there's wasn't a time when he wasn't in trouble.

"What's going on?" I whispered to Julie.

"I don't know. I guess they have to tell us at some point!"

I asked the policemen why they were taking Julie and me in. They explained that they had to take us downtown and clear us.

As they were transporting us to the police department, I started to feel funny. I told the police officers in the front seat that my blood sugar was low. Then I asked them whether they had anything for me to eat.

"We'll let you have something to eat when we get downtown," they promised.

When we got to the station, it came out that Rodney's brother had robbed a jewelry store in Cleveland that had been under police surveillance. So, he was booked.

Meanwhile, Julie and I were in a locked jail cell, waiting to be released. A gorgeous officer came walking up and said to me through the bars, "Miss, I have a candy bar for you."

Julie laughed and said, "Who gets a cop to bring them a candy bar? I guess you can get men to do anything for you!"

To get arrested the first time Julie and I hung out together was memorable, to say the least. We still laugh about it to this day.

We all got released from jail, except Rotten Rodney's brother. He was arrested for robbing the jewelry store in Ohio and then going on the run.

When we got back to Rodney's house, he opened a big hope chest and showed us what was inside. It was full of pot.

"Rodney!" I said. "The cops would have made us *stay* in jail if they'd found that!"

After that, I never again stood on the same piece of real estate as Rodney. Julie ended up staying with him for ten more years. Not surprisingly, Rodney landed in prison for getting into a fight with a cop.

I was in the bank in Clearwater. Out of all the people in there, one guy caught my eye. He was a redhead who looked exactly like Opie Taylor from *The Andy Griffith Show*. His name even turned out to be Andy.

That same week I met Andy, I was in Ollie's Bar. There he was again—all six-feet of him, with his pretty blue eyes and his nice smile. I couldn't stop looking at him. We went on to date for about a year and a half.

One day, Andy said, "You need a real animal, Suzette, instead of that stuffed animal. You need a dog!"

"I love dogs! I've had lots of 'em," I explained.

He got me a dog and I named her Blondie. She was smaller than a mini-poodle—so small she could fit in my purse.

Toward the end of our dating relationship, Andy started hanging out with my dad. That didn't sit well with me at all. As you know by now, Dad was always scamming people and ripping them off. He took advantage of everybody he could.

When I tried to warn Andy away from Dad, he didn't believe me. That came as no surprise. Everyone figured I had to be exaggerating.

One day after not hearing from Andy for a while, I went looking for him at Dad's. I was really hoping I wouldn't find him there, but I had a feeling I would. Sure enough, there was Andy. Dad wasn't there at the moment.

Between Andy not calling me for a while and him turning up at my Dad's, I was done. "That's it!" I said. "I'm leaving."

Just as I opened the door to leave Dad's house, he came in. I saw blood on his clothes and asked him if he was okay.

"I'm alright," he said, "but you should see the other guy!"

Dad told me that some idiot druggie friend of his had pissed him off. So, he stabbed him. Dad described stabbing the guy very casually, like he was telling us about going grocery shopping.

"Well," I said, "I don't know what your deal is with the guy. All I know is that you'd better get in the shower and get that blood off of you! We're leaving."

I was really mad at Andy for having anything to do with my dad. "He's trouble!" I told Andy. "He'll get you put in jail."

I was done with Andy. We spent too much time partying together, and he spent too much time hanging around with Dad. Not only that, but he didn't want any of the things I wanted, including a family. I'd had it.

Toward the end of our relationship, our arguments had gotten more and more heated. At least he never hit me. I knew he probably wanted to hit me plenty of times. Thankfully, he was a real gentleman.

I could really push someone's buttons. One time, I got so mad, I threw some books around the house. It all went back to the anger I had against Dad. All the awful things he had said and done to me were still in my head. They kept rising back up and making me mad.

The other day I found a photo of Andy and me. In the picture, we're standing outside. I'm wearing my beauty-pageant banner, with the words Miss Bikini on it. I'd won two hundred and fifty dollars along with the title. In the photo, my hair was all wet beneath my crown. (As part of winning the Miss Bikini title, I had to do a dunk tank.) Andy had come to the event and was standing beside me in the photo, happy and smiling.

I had finished beauty school—but I didn't take the test to get my license until years later. When I did finally take the test and the results came back, I would find out that I needed to take my state board exam over again. I had failed the chemistry portion of the test, so I retook it. Seven years from the time I started cosmetology in tenth grade, I finally had my cosmetology license.

The modeling school I attended had my number and referred a lot of jobs to me. So did the Motion Picture Association. I did hair and makeup for <u>Tampa Bay Magazine</u> and sometimes I modeled for them, too. And from time to time, I was still working as an extra in movies.

I also auditioned to model a suntanning blanket. The audition involved lying seductively on a blanket on the ground. My friend with big, fake breasts also tried out for the job. That was the only thing she had over me—those breasts.

They chose her and her fake boobs. That didn't surprise me, and it didn't motivate me to want to get a boob job. I did get a job for T.V. doing hair and makeup for models. On one shoot for an Auto Trader UHF T.V. show, the model failed to show up. I happened to fit into her swimsuit. So, they put me in the swimsuit for the show, which ran for half an hour every Saturday.

I didn't like doing that. It was more about my body than my talent. It didn't make me feel good. I was being used to sell classic cars and boats. One time, I was in a lineup with other models, some of whom had big fake boobs. As a way to sell a fishing boat, we were supposed to have a fishing pole between our legs and pull on it.

I was shy and modest by nature and uncomfortable with this kind of sexual messaging. I was so embarrassed to show my body, I hardly ever even wore a swimsuit in public. Once I shot a butt poster with six other girls showing their ass. I made $600 but I didn't like the feeling it gave me. Thankfully, my face wasn't shown so I was able to remain anonymous.

One day, when I went to a convenience store after a shoot, a little African American boy about nine years old tried to sell some crack to me.

I was shocked. "You have to get that out of your hands, and go home!" I told him.

There was something about that moment that shocked me into a decision. It caused me to have an awakening.

I said to myself, *I really need a fresh start! I don't know what I'm doing here in Florida, anyway. I am wearing swimsuits in these shoots that are only about my body and doing T.V. shows I don't want to do.*

I was making plenty of money doing hair and makeup for magazines and on set for movies and T.V. In fact, I was getting so much work, I was turning down people who wanted me to do hair and makeup. But I was not happy with myself. I was at a real crossroads.

Twenty-Eight

THE TURNING POINT came when I got an emergency call from my mom. I figured she must be calling to tell me that Grandma Margaret had died. It turned out to be my cousin Maria's dad, Uncle Eddie, who passed. He and I weren't close.

Even though Uncle Eddie's death didn't hit me hard, it did make me take a second look at my life. It made me realize that the time had come for me to live close to my family again. So, I decided that I would move to Nebraska and start a new life near my mom. I'd been feeling like it was time for a fresh start, anyway, so the timing made sense.

Mom and J.R. had been traveling around the racetrack circuit and then J.R. got injured. He broke both of his legs in an accident. He was already bowlegged from getting knocked off a horse when he was thirty. After the accident, he and Mom got stuck in Nebraska for a year while he recuperated.

In order to move to Nebraska, I needed money to buy a plane ticket. So, I called Dad and told him I wanted to go be with Mom for a while. Dad always had the big money. Sometimes he would bankroll me to help get me somewhere. He paid for my plane ticket and agreed to buy me a dog crate for Blondie.

About the time I arrived in Columbus, Nebraska, I got word that Ricky was getting married to his high school sweetheart—in Florida. He had been in and out of the army and was on leave at the time of the wedding. I had used the money Dad gave me to get myself to Nebraska and was still getting settled. So, I was unable to fly back for my brother's wedding. I was really sad about it but there was nothing I could do about it. I didn't have the money for another plane ticket.

Mom, J.R., and Grandma Margaret all missed the wedding too. The only one who was able to attend was John because he was already in Florida. Mom sent Ricky and his bride a bunch of wedding gifts from all of us. She wanted Ricky to feel like he had his family there with him on his big day.

I decided to take some college courses at Columbus Community College. When I took an admissions test, my reading and math scores were really low. I was having trouble retaining things, whether the subject was math, English, or writing.

I had to get my skills up in order to take college-level classes. So, I was put in remedial classes. I really enjoyed the creative-writing lessons because of the freedom involved in that kind of writing. It didn't require me to be too precise. The teachers at the community college were kind and patient with me and offered support through all my classes.

While I was taking all my college preparation and entry classes to help me get into college-level classes, I was also taking art electives. I loved painting, drawing and photography. I ended up taking so many art classes, the class credits started stacking up without me realizing it.

The school told me, "Suzette, you've got so many credits, you've got a couple of degrees waiting for you in the office. All you have to do is fill out the paperwork!"

I had gotten a certificate in art and had credits toward my A.A. degree. To help pay for my college classes, I was in the work experience program at school.

Then something surprising happened. I got to meet Vice President Dan Quayle as a result of a paper I had written for my public relations class. The vice president was coming to our school to speak and was looking for things to talk about related to our student body. When the school principal sent Mr. Quayle the paper I'd written, he expressed an interest in meeting me.

In addition to getting to meet Dan Quayle, a short story I wrote in my creative writing class won an award and got published in a story collection in Germany. My story was about Julie and me on a cruise ship. To make it more interesting, I gave her false teeth and gave myself a fake eye.

"Now you're published!" said my creative writing teacher.

It was a great feeling.

Everything seemed to be falling into place for me in Nebraska. I met a nice lady who owned a mall, and she told me she had an open space for me to put my hair salon. She offered to finance the salon equipment I would need, with me paying her back weekly. I also had a night job taking care of an elderly lady.

Between the salon and my night job, I was making $1,500 a week. I was pretty proud of myself and my self-esteem was growing. I discovered that it was very cheap to live in Nebraska. I was able to buy my first mobile home on a rent-to-own basis for $1,700. (I also paid $150 a month for the lot rental for the mobile home.) It was flawless but it had been sitting empty for a while. Other than the fact that it needed a toilet, it was beautiful.

Then life took an interesting turn. I was dating a Nebraska guy named Dan and I turned up pregnant. I was so happy. I was thirty years old and ready to have a baby. I hadn't planned to have a baby right at that exact moment, but it happened. I was so excited.

Unfortunately, I ended up with a tubal pregnancy. I lost both the baby and one of my fallopian tubes. The doctor told me that this tubal pregnancy cut my chances of having a baby by fifty percent.

As I was recovering from my lost pregnancy, I discovered that Dan liked to drink and fight—just like my dad. That was nothing new. I often seemed to find myself dating a drinker. I realized the time had come for me to take a break from dating. So, I quit guys for a while. When I wanted something to do, I went with Mom to the racetrack and the bars.

On Saturday mornings, I usually went into work feeling a little bit rough from too much partying the night before. One Saturday, I was in my shop at the mall, doing a customer's hair. Those were the days of perms. It wasn't unusual for me to do three or four long-hair perms a day and do haircuts in between.

The shop was always rocking on Saturdays. I had music playing and dryers going and barely heard the shop phone ringing. When I answered, it was a lady calling from a nursing home.

She said, "Margaret Laikins just passed."

I was in shock and couldn't take in the news. I said, "No, I don't have an appointment for her on the books."

Then it hit me. I heard myself say out loud, "Wait . . . Margaret Laikins? That's my grandma!"

"I know, honey. I'm sorry to tell you, but she passed."

Grandma Margaret had been in a nursing home in Oklahoma. Then, as Grandma's dementia got worse, Mom moved Grandma to Nebraska so she could take care of her. Grandma was constantly leaving lit cigarettes and lighters lying around, so someone had to make sure she was safe. Aunt Peggy had been taking care of her but now it was Mom's turn.

I wanted to run out of the shop and go see my mom, but I couldn't leave. I had perm rods in one lady's hair and a shop full of people.

Late one night, I was out partying and then got on the road to drive home. A cop noticed the way I was driving and started following me. I decided I'd better give him the slip, so I ducked into a lake area. When I did, I hit a guard rail and stopped.

I got out of the car as fast as I could. I knew the police were behind me, so I jumped into the water. I was wearing jeans and high-top sneakers, which wasn't the best outfit for swimming. I can swim well enough not to drown, as long as I am swimming underwater or backwards. I started swimming backwards, and from time to time I would flip over and swim underwater.

When I got about to the middle of the lake, I carefully popped my head out of the water to see if the police were still there. I could see that now, there were even more police around my car.

I was getting tired from all the swimming. And, the Schnapps I had been drinking earlier in the evening was making me nauseous. I felt like I might vomit. I thought to myself, *I've got to get out of here before I drown!*

I wasn't sure whether to try to swim back to the side of the lake where I'd left my car or try to make it to the other side. I was about equal distance from both sides. I figured my best bet was to try to get to the side of the lake where there were no police. So, I backstroked my way across.

Since I was swimming on my back, I was visible. I figured my white t-shirt might give me away, so I took it off and left it in the water. I kept swimming and made it to the other side. I climbed out of the lake and made my way to a ditch where I could take cover. There were mosquitoes and gnats in the air, and they were trying to make a meal out of me.

I crouched down in the ditch. When the coast seemed clear, I ran a few houses down. I saw a big hunter-green bath towel hanging on someone's clothesline. Those are the best towels ever, so soft and warm. I grabbed the towel and wrapped it around me to cover my shirtless chest. Then I worked my way down into another ditch on a side road.

I stayed there for about half an hour. The sun started coming up. By that time, I had sobered up a bit. I knew I was going to have to come clean, and it seemed best to face the trouble head-on. In the cold light of day, facing the authorities didn't seem as daunting. So, when a truckload of worker guys came by. I got them to take me to the police station, and I told my story to an officer.

The police gave me a citation for careless driving. I figured, *That's fine, considering what they could've done to me!*

I realized that even though the move to Nebraska had been a fresh start for me, I'd fallen into some old habits when I got there. Since I didn't know anyone when I first got there, I had lowered my standards and been spending time with whoever was around. I started really working on being the best person I could be, and surrounding myself with the best people I could find.

For starters, that meant being more choosey about my boyfriends. No more drinking-and-fighting guys for me. I had already reached the point where I was done fighting with my brothers. I wanted to treasure the time together while we had it. I had lost interest in aggravating them like I'd done for so many years when I was young.

Ricky grew up to love and appreciate me, his big sister. He even wrote me a beautiful poem. John and I have also grown close and share a love of cars and music.

I had been buying and selling trailers. Now I had possession of all these trailers—but what I really wanted was a baby. I was out of sorts with myself.

Around this time, Dad started coming around again. One day, he managed to convince J.R. to get into a car with him.

"Come on," said Dad. "Let's you and me go have some drinks."

I don't know what possessed J.R. to get into a car with Dad—a conman who could talk just about anybody into just about anything. Dad took J.R. to a bar and stayed there just long enough to get him good and drunk.

Then, Dad put J.R. back in the car, drove him down a dark road and pulled over. He told J.R., "Now, get out and start running!"

J.R. was only five-foot-five but he was fast. He took off running for his life.

Dad cocked his .357 Magnum, the long-barrel gun he always carried on him. (As a little kid, I was always amazed to see such a huge gun.)

Dad shot off the gun as J.R. was running through the cornfields. He was trying to scare J.R. and make him feel like he might kill him. That was Dad. He liked to scare a person half to death, just to prove that he could take them out if he wanted to. Then he'd reel them back in, as if the person was supposed to feel grateful that Dad has spared their life. When I heard what Dad had done, I was really mad at him.

The first time Dad came to Nebraska, Mom left and went to Florida.

We all thought she was leaving J.R. and going back to Dad. It wasn't that at all. She was just trying to shake Dad off her trail. She flew down to Florida and then turned around and flew back to Nebraska really quickly. The only thing was, eventually Dad followed her back. I never found out what happened during those couple of days.

Sometime afterward, I flew there myself. I felt like I needed to go home to Florida. While I was there, I saw Dad's house and his stripper girlfriend. As part of my efforts to become the best person I could be, I decided to try to forgive Dad for all the ways he had hurt me throughout my life.

So, I sat down and wrote him a long, beautiful letter. I left it behind for him to read, and then I came home to Nebraska.

When Dad got the letter, he called Mom and said, "There's no way Suzette could have written that letter. It's too well put together. You must have written it."

That made me really mad. Dad had put me through so much as a child, and I was trying to work through it instead of harboring hate against him. Instead of appreciating the effort I was making, Dad attributed my efforts to Mom.

What a waste of time! I said to myself.

After that, I didn't see Dad for a while. He and John were in Colorado on a construction job.

Around that same time, I was in a bar, playing pool in a skirt. As I bent over to take my shots, the bartender noticed a biker standing behind me, taking pictures up my skirt with a Polaroid camera.

When the bartender told me what was happening, I called the guy over to where I was standing. The guy was about six feet tall or six-foot-two. I took my pool cue, which I was holding in my right hand, and cracked it once really hard on the side of his face. When I hit him, his whole head swung to the other side. Then I hit him on that side too. Each time I hit him, I got him with the metal ring on the pool cue. The biker fell over onto the bar, shocked beyond belief.

Then I looked around and realized I'd just clobbered a biker in a bar filled with bikers. I knew that if I didn't get out of there pretty quickly, I'd be in trouble. So, I went to my mom's to hide out.

J.R. came up with the idea to do a little bit of reconnaissance at the bar. So, he went down there and listened for any chatter about me. It turned out that the biker I hit was looking for me—to apologize! He had total respect for me because I had stuck up for myself. I found out from J.R. that the biker's entire face looked beat up and I'd given him a black eye.

While I was growing up, I took a lot of shit, so I had to fight. I was taught to stick up for myself and be scrappy. It helped having a great-grandfather who was a professional fighter. And Grandma Margaret taught me to put up my fists and stick up for myself.

There were times when I felt like a victim, and that paralyzed me. When I did fight back, I quickly found out I was capable of defending myself. I had skills. I had taken a few karate classes with John while we were growing up. And there were those times when John would hold a pillow and have me kick it.

After all the times I'd already been beat up and hurt, I was left feeling like, *No matter how much you hit me or hurt me, you can't hurt me as much as I've already been hurt!* Once you've already been hurt as much as I have, there is nowhere to go from there. I used a mind-over-matter technique to get through painful times.

There is still a little sadistic part of me that likes a good fight, a little pushing, a little back and forth. My adrenaline gets pumping and my face gets red. I get excited over the chance for a good fight. I know how to get people when they're not expecting it and I know how to run. I figure I'll get you before you get me. Then I'm out of there.

TWENTY-NINE

M Y CUSTOMERS SOMETIMES brought their kids with them to the salon. I had a deep longing for kids of my own—but I didn't really want a man. I knew I wasn't good at romantic relationships. My choices in men weren't always the best. And, I often ended up in fights with the men I chose.

I just wanted to have a baby. I figured, *I'm secure financially. I have my own shop. I can take care of a baby.*

I still had the salon space I owned in the mall. When I started thinking more about the future, I realized I'd be better off owning a free-standing location. One of my clients happened to own a baseball-card shop on the main road into town. It was located in a building that had been sitting empty. I noticed it as I passed by every day on my way into the salon.

They did a lease-to-own arrangement for me. It was nice to own both the salon and the property where it was located. In my salon, I sold so much Paul Mitchell product, I got to meet Paul Mitchell himself two or three times. They were quick meet-and-greet occasions where we exchanged a few words and took a photo together. It was great getting to meet him. I had always looked up to him and admired how he'd built a successful business with only a seven-hundred-dollar initial investment.

I'd had two hair stylists working for me at my salon in the mall. The plan was that both of them would come with me to the new salon. But, one of my two former employees stayed behind, and did me dirty. Instead of sending my longtime customers over to the new shop when they called and asked about me, he simply said "Oh, she's not here but I can take care of you."

I also lost customers when I moved to the new salon because they never received the mailer I sent out, letting them know about the new location. So, it was a double whammy.

I replaced the betrayer stylist with someone else. Over time, I added various stylists who rotated in and out of the shop. At one point, I had about seven stylists working for me. That was five too many. Over time, the two best ones stayed with me. Two turned out to be the magic number.

Since I was starting over in a new location, my income dropped from $1,500 a week to $700. Most of the customers at the new shop were walk-ins, not longstanding customers I had known for years.

I was no longer bringing in extra income at night either. I had been looking after elderly people in the evenings before I moved to the new salon, but working so many hours had gotten to be too much. I put all my attention into the new shop, fixing up the building I'd bought. I put in new floors, put on a new roof, and made other improvements to bring the shop up to code.

Since I had decided to have a baby on my own, I was going to have to start the ball rolling on my own. So, Mom and I took a trip to the University of Nebraska to look at the book of sperm donors.

Right as I was planning to become a single mom with the help of a sperm donor, I met a guy named Nels. I saw him first at the racetrack. Then, I was at a bar one night, playing pool (and winning), and I saw this handsome guy walk by.

It was Nels again. I said, "You have the biggest nose I've ever seen!"

He smiled at me—a smile so big and beautiful, I was hooked.

Nels was Swedish with white blonde, curly hair he wore short on the sides. While we were dating, he sang me Elvis love songs, and we fell in love.

Around the time I met him, I sold all my trailers and moved into the back room of my shop. It was all the room I needed. Lucky for me, the place was zoned for residential as well as commercial use. Nels began staying with me at my shop. That's when it came to light that he enjoyed partying more than I did at that point in my life.

Nels earned his living at the racetrack, training horses for their owners—but the income was spotty. That bothered me, but I chalked it up to the fact that he was only twenty-six. I thought that maybe he was struggling because he was four years younger than me and less mature. I was hoping it was just a phase he was going through.

One day, I told him, "I really want a baby!"

"I can take care of that!" he said.

So, we got busy trying to get me pregnant. I told myself, "If it happens, it happens." I remembered what the doctor had told me after my tubal pregnancy. It lowered my odds by fifty percent.

Nels asked me to marry him and started looking at rings. I didn't see marriage as a positive thing, and I wasn't looking to marry anybody. It had taken me that many years to even think about becoming a mother, much less getting married. I knew that I had a hot temper from all the abuse I had suffered. I figured I would have my hands full with being a good mother and business owner. Adding marriage into the equation seemed like tempting fate.

Finally, I relented and told him we could talk about the possibility of marriage. But when I got into a marriage mindset, I started taking a second look at Nels. There were certain ways in which I needed him to step up if he wanted to become my husband.

I told Nels that if he wanted to get married, I wanted to see him get a real job and come up with the money to help support me and the baby I was hoping to have with him. I had always brought in steady income and I felt like he should too. Any income he did bring in at the racetrack went toward expenses related to the horses he trained.

He let go of his horses and agreed to get a stable job. Every morning, he left for work, and returned home in the evening. This went on for about a month.

Something in my gut told me that he wasn't really going to work.

So, I told my mother that I was suspicious and asked her if she would follow Nels to work one morning. Mom agreed and followed Nels right to the racetrack.

After that, there was a lot of drama between us. I threw Nels' things out the back door of my shop but I didn't leave him. Instead, he and I ended up moving into a little duplex across the street. (The back of my shop was too small for us, since we were hoping that I would soon be pregnant.)

While Nels and I were living across the street from my shop, I thought I might be pregnant. I wanted to take a pregnancy test when I was alone. I waited for my moment, took the test, and held my breath. And there it was—a positive result!

I was so excited. I picked up the phone and called my friend, Gwen. I wanted to tell her first. Then I called my mom and told her. And *then* I called Nels. My excitement didn't last long. Pretty quickly, I started feeling sick, sick, sick.

Around this time, I found out that Dad was headed to Nebraska. He'd been gone for a while. During that time, I had made real progress in my life. I didn't want Dad to undermine that by returning to Nebraska.

He had a way of knocking me off kilter. He would make jokes at my expense, call me dumb or stupid, and tell me that my donut wasn't all the way glazed. That was the last insult I remember getting from him. The news that he was coming back hit me so hard, I started shaking and dropped the phone. I felt like I was having a convulsion.

Before Dad had left town the last time, he was running around with my friend, Michelle. The next thing I knew, Michelle started taking prescription drugs with Dad, and lying to her husband about it. She became such a mess, I couldn't be friends with her anymore. I was really mad at Dad for taking away my friend.

Dad was also coming by our apartment and picking up Nels. Right before Dad got back into town, Nels had been trying to get a handle on his partying. He seemed to be doing really well and going to work. (Or, as far as I knew, anyway.)

Then Nels started staying out all night with Dad. I woke up one morning in the little duplex, and I was all by myself. I realized that Nels was still out with Dad. I got mad and put his things out in the yard. I told him I was leaving him, and then went over to Mom's to tell her the news.

When I got back, I found all of *my* belongings in a pile. On top of the pile was a pair of baby shoes. Things got messy between us as I tried to leave him. This time, the anger stuck around even after the fighting was over. That was the first time I had ever fought with anyone and had it stick. In my experience, people fought and then they made up.

I had come to the conclusion that we had no future. I was uncomfortable with the age difference between us and wasn't sure he was ready for fatherhood. So, we broke up for good.

Things weren't really working out for Nels in Nebraska, either. So, Dad took him back to Minnesota to be with his family. He knew that Nels was hurting over our breakup and needed the love and support of his family around him. The fact that Dad thought he was doing right by me when he took Nels back to Minnesota didn't occur to me until years later. At the time, I was just plain mad.

I was upset with Nels for leaving me, and mad at Dad for helping him leave. I had assumed that, even though we were broken up, we would at least be friends. I was counting on Nels being there for the baby.

For three or four weeks after Nels left, I was as sick as a dog. Being sick and upset at the time same wasn't good for me or the baby.

I had a customer who kept telling me, "I've got this farmer friend and he's single . . ."

I thought to myself, *What's with all the farmers?*

When I first moved to Nebraska, I was introduced to a cattle man. He would feed cattle and take them to slaughter. I refused to date a cow executioner. I love animals and don't even like to eat beef.

Then I realized that I was living in such a rural community, of course I was going to end up dating farmers. There was no way around it. So,

I agreed to go out with that customer's farmer friend. When the guy showed up to take me to dinner, he was wearing a trucker's cap.

I refused to go on a second date with the guy. My customer said, "But he's a rich farmer!"

"I don't care who he is!" I said. "When I go out to dinner with a man, I want to sit at a table with a gentleman. Who wears a cap to dinner?"

Then the nail tech in my salon suggested I create a personal ad. I liked the idea and had fun writing the ad. I described myself as a green-eyed, blonde, sexy, sassy non-smoker. I did leave out one small detail—my pregnancy. I planned to wait to reveal that fact until someone seeing the ad was truly interested.

When someone was interested in my ad, they would call a voicemail number assigned specifically to me. In my outgoing message, I said, "Hi, I'm Suzette, and I'm Polish-Irish, self-employed, very independent, outspoken . . . and pregnant. If you would like a date with me, tell me a little about yourself, and leave your number."

When I checked my voicemail, I heard a lot of clicks. Those were the guys who hung up when they heard the part about me being pregnant. On one of the voicemails, the guy had a very calm voice. Being hyper myself, I have always been attracted to calm people.

I called the calm guy back. He turned out to be a farmer from a town called Schuyler. He sounded really nice over the phone. So, I told him I would go out with him, and would call him back to tell him when.

The very same day that I left that message for the farmer from Schuyler, my friend Cathy came into my shop. I had cut her hair for years. She said, "You don't really want to have a baby without a father in the picture, Suzette. The baby's going to need a father."

"Oh, yes, I do! Just watch me."

"Listen," she said, "my sister, Lisa, is married to this guy, Larry. He has a brother named Terry. You should be with him. At least go out with him and give him a chance."

I was surprised by how sure she was that I belonged with the guy. "What does he do?" I asked.

"He's a farmer," said Cathy.

I said to myself, *Well, I'm already planning to date the farmer from Schuyler. I might as well go on a date with this guy first.*

"Okay, I'll go. But you have to come too!"

She couldn't join us, so she sent her sister, Lisa and Lisa's husband, Larry.

THIRTY

O N THE NIGHT of the date, Lisa and Larry picked me up. We
got a table and waited for Terry to arrive. I raised my eyes and
watched him walk into the restaurant. I saw his broad shoulders
and eyes so green, they glowed. This man was such a specimen, the light
shone around him.

Green eyes have always been my favorite, and Terry has the most
beautiful green eyes I have ever seen in my life. Not only that, but his
glowing green eyes are wolfen, like those of a husky. I was so excited
to meet this man who was big and strong and tall, with gorgeous eyes.
Best of all, he wasn't wearing a farmer's cap.

Terry took a seat on my right side and hardly spoke at all. Having
him sit by my side worked well for me. His positioning allowed me to
keep from staring at him. I was so affected by his presence, I wanted to
avoid looking right at him. Just like people are told not to look directly
into the light of the sun.

Lisa was very quiet but, thankfully, Larry kept the conversation
going. He showed nice, polite interest in me and asked me questions
about myself. When he found out that I liked to fly and was actually in
the process of getting my pilot's license, he talked to me about flying. If
he hadn't kept talking, there would have been a lot of awkward silence
at the table.

Terry barely said two words to me the entire time we were sitting
there. That didn't matter to me. I was so taken with him, my stomach
was bubbling from nerves.

When everyone finished eating, I stood up, and said, "I'm going to go."

Terry pulled out my chair for me, walked me out to my car, and opened my door for me. He was a true Nebraska man—almost as sweet as a southern man and twice as tough. He was very chivalrous, but he was a man of few words.

I got in my car and turned the key to drive away.

He was polite and said, "Goodbye and thank you" but he didn't give me even a hint of what he had thought of me.

I had met plenty of men who were too eager, so Terry was a nice breath of fresh air. I found him to be intriguing and mysterious. He looked to me like something right off the cover of a romance novel— big, strong, and tanned. I was so attracted to him, it was crazy. (And, I still am to this day!)

I went back to work and went about my normal routine. Days passed and I didn't hear a word from Terry. Meanwhile, the farmer from Schuyler kept calling me. I couldn't have cared less. I really liked Terry and wanted another date with him.

About ten days went by with no word from Terry. I asked myself, *Does he not like me? Or does he think maybe I wouldn't go out with him again? Or is he just busy?*

Then Cathy came in to buy a bottle of shampoo. "How did you like the date?" she asked me.

"I loved it! I really like him, but he hasn't called me. Do you know what happened? Does he not like me?"

"I don't know. I'll check it out and see if he liked you."

The next day when I got into work, there was a big bouquet of flowers waiting for me. There was also a little stuffed mama bunny with a baby bunny as part of the arrangement. The card said something about him being sorry he hadn't called earlier, but he had gotten busy.

He knows I'm pregnant but he doesn't care! I said to myself. I was relieved.

About ten minutes after the flowers and stuffed animal arrived, the phone rang. It was Terry. He explained that he had been busy planting crops.

Then he said, "I'd love to take you on another date. What do you want to do?"

I had an idea. "What about the car show coming up in Omaha?"

Omaha was two hours away—the perfect length of a car ride for me to find out whether Terry could stand my gabbing. I once dated a guy who asked me whether I ever shut up. So, I needed to find out whether Terry could deal with me before I let myself start liking him too much.

The ride to the car show was fun. Terry picked me up in his bright red truck with fancy pinstriping along the side panels. I was never much of a truck girl, but this was a beautiful, expensive pickup truck. It was fun riding high up off the ground with him.

I did most of the talking. I told Terry about my family life, and what it was like being raised with two brothers. I told him how that made me a bit of a tomboy.

Terry didn't seem too bothered by my gabbiness. He did a little bit of talking himself. He told me about his first car—a Trans Am with the big bird on the front. That is one of my favorite cars.

"I still have it," he said. "It's sitting in the garage."

When Terry told me that he had five sisters, I thought, *Oh, so that's why being around a girl who's talkative is nothing to him! He's used to hearing a girl talk.*

Terry also told me that he had three brothers. Between the four boys and five girls, there were nine kids in his family.

When we got to the car show, we talked about cars and had fun. Despite the fact that I was clearly and obviously pregnant, the baby was the one topic of discussion that never came up.

By about three months into our dating relationship, Terry had met my family. There were more members of his family to meet, so I was meeting them along the way. On the weekends, I went to Terry's family farm. He lived in a small two-bedroom mobile home on the farm. Lisa, Larry and their kids were occupying the main house, where Terry grew up.

One time when I got there, Terry had a book waiting for me. It was about all the things to expect when you're pregnant. Terry caught on pretty quickly that I was not a big reader. He rolled with it and didn't seem thrown off by it. He would open the book and read aloud to me.

I thought it was so sweet of him to read to me. My heart also melted when I saw him pick up his tiny little nephew (Larry's son, Austin) and carry him around.

All the things the book said to expect at different milestones of pregnancy were coming true right before our eyes. He would read, for example, that at week eight my appetite would increase. Sure enough, I got to week eight and suddenly, I couldn't get enough to eat.

I was still being very cautious and careful, observing everything Terry did. I was truly sick of men by this point. I only wanted to date someone if I was fairly sure we were going to end up together.

I was sizing up Terry, asking myself, *Is he good enough? Is he strong enough? Is he everything I need and want?* I had him under a microscope. I wondered if Terry was also sizing me up. He showed no signs of it, but I figured he was probably doing the same thing on his end.

A couple of weeks into our relationship, Terry came to my shop at the end of the day to pick me up. As we were getting ready to leave the salon, I went to shut off the lights. As I did so, I leaned in close to Terry.

Standing so close to him, my heart started to beat really fast, and my face got hot. I had to have him. I leaned up toward his face, grabbed the back of his head, and pulled him down toward me. (He is much taller than I am.)

He wrapped both of his strong arms around my back, pulled me close and tight, and kissed me. The feeling of his big rough hands around my waist took my breath away and gave me goosebumps.

By now, I had realized that Terry was the man for me. He was a family man, he was kind, and our chemistry was passionate and electric. I was seriously into Terry, and twenty years later, that hasn't changed.

In many ways, we are complete opposites. I have always been happiest when I'm on the go. Terry, on the other hand, is most comfortable on the farm. Any time he goes into town or does anything outside his comfort zone, he gets anxiety. If he had his way, he would spend all his time on the farm.

Any time he agrees to leave his comfort zone, I feel really special. The few times he has ever gotten onto a plane with me, I've felt so special, I want to jump on him. I know what it takes for him to do these things, and I know he's doing them to make me happy. He would just as soon stay home.

The longer Terry and I dated, the more he included me in the family. He also began to refer to my baby as part of the family, and that felt really good. I am all about my family. When I am not by myself, I am with my family. I am rarely with anyone else.

When I saw how family-oriented and family-focused Terry was, I knew for sure that he was the one. He really lived for his family, and that was something I wanted for myself. Terry was self-employed, like a lot of the men I had dated, but much more family-oriented than the others.

When I met Terry's mom, I worried that there was no way I could ever live up to her standards. She was so put together, and her house was so proper and perfect, she seemed like the perfect mom. That made me a little bit nervous. I was also worried that she might object to her son dating a pregnant woman.

Thankfully, she took to me right away and we really hit it off. She even wrote a beautiful letter for me to keep in a scrapbook. Unfortunately, other members of Terry's family weren't sure what to make of me at first.

Terry was always busy. But, since he runs his own schedule, he was able to make time for me. I was happy to see that he made me a priority. If he hadn't been able to do that, I wouldn't have wanted to be with him.

I was busy myself, working weekdays from 9:00 in the morning to 9:00 at night at the salon. I was also training to be a Paul Mitchell educator on the weekends. We struck the perfect balance, making each other a priority without smothering each other.

We saw each other when we could, and things flowed along pretty smoothly for a year and a half. We were from two different worlds, so that caused a little bit of friction between us from time to time. He had grown up on the family farm and I was a city girl who liked pretty things. It took some time to learn each other's ways and adapt.

THIRTY-ONE

THE CLOSER IT got to my due date, the more uncomfortable I felt, and the fatter I got. I started thinking about giving birth and realized I needed to get my own place. I was still living in the back room of my salon. I knew that was no place bring a baby. (I had given up the duplex and moved back into my shop after Nels left town.)

So, I got a place with a former roommate named Steve. He was the best roommate ever. The only thing he did was sleep there. He was up at four in the morning and in bed by seven at night. I was never home, myself. I was usually either at the salon or at Terry's. I needed to save even more money, so I got a second roommate and rented the basement to him. I felt like one of the guys.

One day, Terry took me to his mom's house. When we got there, he said, "Come down into the basement with me for a minute. I need to get something."

We went downstairs into the finished basement where Terry had lived for the first nine years of his life. While I was admiring the basement, Terry got down on one knee, opened up a black velvet ring box, and presented me with a ring.

I had known that the proposal was coming but that didn't make me any less excited. Terry barely got the words "Will you marry me?" out of his mouth before I grabbed the ring and ran upstairs.

I'm not even sure I kissed him first. I couldn't wait to share the news with his mom. Terry came upstairs after me. When I showed Terry's mom the ring, she smiled.

About two weeks later, Terry said to me, "You never answered me, you know."

"What? Oh, yes, yes, of course I'll marry you! Sorry about that. I just loved that ring so much."

During the time we were dating, we talked about life. That's how I got to know Terry and his five thousand acres. He knew the land like the back of his hand. He would put me in the tractor and let me sit with him while he was planting the corn. I was barely pregnant at the time, and my little belly would bounce up and down as the tractor crawled through the bumpy fields.

It sometimes took Terry all night to plant the corn. Farmers figure that the sooner the corn gets in the ground, the better. They are always working against the elements and trying to dodge the spring rains. During all-night corn planting, Terry and I would listen to country music in the moonlight.

It is catastrophic for the snows to come before all the corn gets harvested. When the corn gets wet despite Terry's best efforts to prevent it, it must be dried with special dryers before it can be sold. So, at harvest time, Terry gets up in the morning, feeds the cattle, and stays on that tractor until he can't ride anymore. When he gets too exhausted, he sometimes sleeps in the shed by the field. Weather runs a farmer's life, so it also runs the life of a farmer's wife.

I was very afraid of marrying Terry. It was nothing personal—I was just afraid of marrying anyone. I knew that he was raised Catholic and was very religious. So, it made sense that he wanted to be married. I, on the other hand, would have been fine just being with him and the baby without getting married. I didn't want to be tied to him for life if the marriage didn't work out.

I dragged out our engagement while I watched Terry very carefully. If I *was* going to marry him, I first needed to find out what kind of father he would be. Finally, I felt confident that he would be a good father to my baby. Now, it was time to start planning our wedding.

Daddy John gave me eight hundred dollars for the wedding. It was the right and proper thing for him to do, and it made me feel good. I knew I was going to need the money for the big wedding we had planned. I was expected to pay for anyone I invited to the wedding. That included the invitations, the decorations, and the dress. I planned to invite thirty-five people to the wedding. Terry invited three hundred people.

On September 28th, 1995, I went into labor and went to the hospital. After I was in labor for thirty-two hours, my doctors realized they were going to need to do a C-section. Terry stayed with me the entire time, holding my hand. When the doctor gave me the C-Section, my big, strong farmer nearly passed out.

On September 29th, I gave birth to my wonderful twenty-two-inch baby boy. Suddenly, the nurse yelled a hospital code to the other medical staff. Then she ran out of the room carrying my son, who was dangerously blue! They were worried about his oxygen levels.

So, I didn't get to hold my baby right away. While I was waiting for the nurse to return with my baby, I started trying on names for size.

It was everything I could do to keep my eyes open. I kept wondering, *When am I going to get to sleep?* I had been in labor for thirty-two hours—and I was up the entire day before I went into labor.

The nurse brought back my baby and put him in my arms. He was all cleaned up and was crying. I knew that was a good sign. I didn't think he looked that much better, but he did have a little bit of color in his cheeks.

"He's going to be fine," explained the nurse. "We aren't sure why he wasn't getting enough oxygen."

It was time to name the baby. I had planned on naming him Chevy because I like cars so much. And I knew that Chevy Chase had that name, so I wouldn't be the first one to come up with it.

Mom drove me home from the hospital. (Terry was out at the farm, working at the time.) She said, "You know, if you give your child an odd name, he will always have trouble in life. He'll be defensive and have trouble getting jobs and promotions. It will cause him nothing but problems. You can't name the baby Chevy."

I knew that my mom was right, but I struggled to come up with another boy's name I liked. The only other name I liked was John Paul, as in John Paul deJoria, the cofounder of Paul Mitchell hair products. And, Pope John Paul II. And both my brother John and my birth father, Daddy John, shared the name John.

While I was in the hospital, I had been saying Our Father prayers and praying to Pope John Paul. I thought the pope was awesome. I admired and respected John Paul DeJoria from Paul Mitchell. And I love my brother John. So that settled it. I decided to name my son Jon Paul. (I wanted my son's first name to be somewhat unique, so I used the Jon spelling, rather than John.)

I asked my mom to pull into the Walmart parking lot so I could run in and get some photos taken of the baby. I took seven shots in a row, with me proud as pie, holding my baby. Then the baby started to cry— and I started to panic.

This was my first time holding, rocking, or feeding an infant all by myself. Up until then, the nurses had been holding him, or were nearby while I cradled the baby in my arms in the hospital bed. I didn't even know what time the nurses had given the baby his last bottle.

In the photos taken after my son started crying, my face shows my emotions. I was cringing and scared because I didn't know what to do with a crying baby. The photos were mixed—me looking happy and proud and me looking terrified.

Unfortunately, I ended up with a bad infection in the C-section incision a couple of weeks after giving birth. I felt awful and nearly died. The baby wasn't happy either. He cried constantly. He ended up back in the hospital at ten weeks old with pneumonia, colic, and sinus problems.

Being so sick myself, it was hard to take care of a sick baby. I had a babysitter helping me out quite a bit. Steve, one my two roommates, also helped. He happened to be a father of six, so he had experience with kids. While I was sick, he would rock the baby for a few hours here and there. That way, I could get some sleep. I was toughing it out and doing my thing.

I didn't want to marry Terry immediately after giving birth. Terry didn't care whether we got married before or after the baby was born.

He would have preferred that we get married beforehand, but he didn't insist.

During the entire time we were dating, Terry never tried to control me. That was one of the things that won me over about him. I didn't want the input of any man on how I should raise my child.

We would end up having Jon Paul's first birthday in our house after we'd gotten married. When it came to our wedding plans, Terry liked to keep things simple. I started to realize that he was very traditional and frugal. The fact that I was marrying a farmer really started to sink in.

I assumed that we would both live in his mobile home after we were married. Then, one weekend as we were driving back from town where we had been shopping or something, Terry said something that surprised me.

"Look there," I said, "somebody's building a house right off the highway."

"Actually, that's *our* house!" he said.

"Our house? I thought we were going to live in the mobile home!"

Instead of being happy over the surprise, I was mad at Terry. I couldn't believe that he had planned out where we were going to live without any input from me. He didn't talk to me about any of my preferences.

Our house was built on the family land. They owned five thousand acres over three counties. When Terry told me with great pride of ownership, "That's our land," my feeling was, *Yeah, whatever!*

As far as I was concerned, having so much land meant that Terry would have to work like a mule to help look after it all. That was fine with him. He lived to work. But not me—I wanted to live our lives and have fun. I also worried that working so hard would be a death sentence for a man with diabetes.

Terry making the house decision without me wasn't a dealbreaker. I already had so much invested in him. I had already sold my shop, given up my business, given up my home, and spent every dime on the wedding. I had no money, no income stream, and no place to live.

In my determination to enter the marriage debt-free, I had even declared bankruptcy. I took care of what bills I could, and filed bankruptcy on the rest. I didn't like having to do it but I figured, *It's okay. Nobody dies from declaring bankruptcy.*

I'd been willing to give up everything prior to the marriage because I knew I would be living a much better life after we were married. I also knew that I could and would start all over if I had to. Ever since I was young, I'd had a job or my own business, and I'd always earned my own money.

Twenty-two days before our wedding, I got another surprise. Terry handed me a document and said, "I need you to sign this prenup."

"I'm not signing that!"

"If you don't sign it, there will be no wedding."

While we were dating, the subject of a prenup had come up. I told Terry that I had asked for a prenup from my baby's father. I also told him that I believed in prenups as a way for both the husband and the wife to protect the businesses they had built. But I thought that Terry and I were going to sit down *together* and come up with prenup terms that were acceptable to us both.

Instead, he had the prenup drawn up without my input and then presented me with it. I felt totally blindsided. Now I was in a terrible position. I knew that Terry's family would call off the wedding if I refused to sign the prenup. And, I had people coming in from out of town to attend the wedding.

"Well, if you don't like this document, what *do* you want?" asked Terry.

Terry wanted to be with me. He was invested in our relationship. And thankfully, he was willing to negotiate. He's not a my-way-or-the-highway kind of guy. We talked things over. He agreed to put some things in the prenup that were to my benefit. It felt good knowing that I had been smart enough to insist upon certain things on my own behalf. I was taking care of myself.

I had learned from my mother, who never did look after herself very well in her marriage to Dad. She was full of grace and as sweet as pie, and I wanted to be just like her. But the things I had seen Dad put her through during their marriage stayed with me. I didn't want to suffer the same fate.

It was time to decide who was going to walk me down the aisle. I really wanted Dad on one side of me and J.R. on the other. But Dad didn't like that idea one bit. As far as he was concerned, he was my dad, he had raised me, and he should be the only one walking me down the aisle. He was also mad over the fact that I'd agreed to sign the prenup.

Dad never went to get his tux sized. Instead, he and John left town and went to South Dakota for a construction job. By this point, I was tired of all the drama Dad had put me through over the wedding.

I said to myself, *Forget this! I'll just have Ricky walk me down the aisle.*

Ricky had just finished nursing school at the time. He had gotten his tux and everything was shaping up nicely for the big day.

THIRTY-TWO

TERRY AND I were married at St. Anthony's Catholic Church in Columbus, Nebraska. On the day of my wedding, I was really nervous. I worried that Terry's family might not completely accept me as part of the family. We came from such different backgrounds.

I was watching the clock and wishing Mom would get to the church already. I had ordered only a few roses from the florist, so I would have some flowers to hand out. All the rest of the flower arrangements were made by my creative mom. She made the bouquets and the corsages. She even made the arrangements for the sides of the pews and big lace bows. At the last minute, she rushed in carrying boxes of flowers and looking absolutely beautiful.

Once Mom arrived, I felt so much better. I was ready to marry Terry. I was wearing a big, poufy Princess Bride wedding dress. I had initially picked out a simple, plain dress. Every few months, Mom and I went back to the store to try it on. Each time, I would gradually try on bigger and bigger dresses. I finally decided on the Princess Bride dress. After working hard to lose my pregnancy weight, I had slimmed down enough to fit into my dress.

I walked down the aisle, with Ricky by my side. I had demoted Dad to a wedding guest since walking me down the aisle didn't work out. I expected him to show up, but I didn't really want him there. I was afraid of the drama that he might bring with him to the church. If someone looked at him sideways, a fight could have broken out. You just never knew what might happen when Dad was around. I was so fed up with him. He never did show up for the wedding.

My brother John made it back to town in time for the wedding, but he stayed in the background. It was just as well, considering his hot temper. I knew that if he found himself in the middle of any drama, he too could end up in a fight with somebody. The last thing I needed on my wedding day was Dad or John getting into a fight.

All eyes were on me as I walked toward Terry, who waited for me at the altar. I've always found it embarrassing to have people looking at me. It was making me nervous. (I felt that way even when I was doing pageants. In fact, that was one of the reasons I got into doing beauty pageants. I had hoped it would help make me less-self-conscious. Unfortunately, that anxious feeling never went away.)

During my pregnancy, a lot of people had said to me, "You're so lucky to have Terry willing to take on that baby!"

I would say, "It's really sexist of you to say that! I think he's lucky to have *us* in his life!"

When it came time for the ceremony, Terry said his vows in a voice that was clear and beautiful. It was so sweet. When it was my turn, I started crying so hard, Terry could hardly understand what I was saying. I cried through the rest of the ceremony. I was a combination of happy, sad, and stressed out.

As I said, I had never really wanted to get married. I'd had my reasons. For one thing, I had always thought that maybe I was too sassy and headstrong to be anyone's wife. Secondly, marriages never seemed meant to last. Marriage just didn't seem like a sensible thing to do.

Now, here I was, exchanging vows with Terry. I was so happy to be marrying him but filled with uncertainty at the same time. I felt like I was losing all my independence and giving up everything I had worked so long and hard to achieve.

By the time the wedding was over, I was exhausted but happy. I felt like it was a new beginning for me—but I still felt drained. The reception was wonderful but also exhausting. There is a tradition in Nebraska for the wedding party to go to a bar for shots and drinks while the guests are gathering at the reception. Sometimes, the wedding party would get a buzz going at the bar and then go to Walmart and push the bride around in a shopping cart. Thank goodness they didn't do that with me.

Our guests were waiting for us at the Eagle's Club banquet hall behind my house. I didn't want to spend time at the bar when I knew that everyone was waiting for us. All I wanted to do was go spend time with my family and the thirty-five guests I had invited. But I went along with the tradition and tried to go with the flow.

Afterwards, we went to the Eagle's Club and took a seat at the head table. We said a prayer and ate our meal. No one raised a glass or made a toast to us. That seemed a bit odd to me but what could I do?

As the guests I had invited finished eating, we cut the cake and served everyone. And then the dancing started. Terry and I did our first dance to a song I picked out: *Forever and Ever, Amen* by Randy Travis (Written by Don Schlitz and Paul Overstreet):

"*. . . As sure as I live, this love that I give*
Is gonna be yours until the day that I die,
Oh, baby, I'm gonna love you forever,
Forever and ever, amen.
As long as old men sit and talk about the weather,
As long as old women sit and talk about old men,
If you wonder how long I'll be faithful,
I'll be happy to tell you again,
I'm gonna love you forever and ever,
Forever and ever, amen . . ."

Once Terry and I finished dancing, I decided to make the quick walk to my house so I could change my shoes. (I was living just across the alleyway from the reception hall, in the house with Steve and the other roommate.) When I got to the house, I decided to lie down. I was exhausted from the festivities.

I fell fast asleep and slept right through the rest of my wedding reception. Terry never woke me up. He just partied with the wedding guests until three in the morning. Then he came and woke me up, saying, "It's time to go home now."

He drove us to our new house, and we spent our first night there. When we walked in the door, I saw that it was filled with furniture. His family had said they were going furniture shopping for us, and I had not objected. They had made it clear that this was their family tradition—for them to pick out the furniture. I was not invited.

Once I saw the furniture with my own eyes, it was a bit of a shock. I was grateful it was all new furniture. But nothing about the furniture, the decorations, or the colors was to my liking or my taste. I figured I could always swap out anything I didn't like later.

When I had said I wanted to paint the inside of the house, Terry's parents made it clear they wanted me to leave it white. Where I came from, the bride always got her way. It wasn't like that in Nebraska. The bride was expected to follow tradition and go along with the way everyone usually did things. It reminded me of the British monarchy, where all the royals are expected to follow protocol. I figured there was no point in fighting city hall, so to speak.

Shortly after we woke up the next morning, Terry's entire family came over. They were there to watch us open each and every card and gift. They had planned to make a note of who sent each gift and card, and the amount of every monetary gift we received. Terry's mom wanted to make sure she knew how much everyone had given so she could thank them too.

The only thing was, as we were leaving the reception the night before, Terry and I opened all the cards and mixed up all the money. Since the money was out of the cards, nobody ever knew who gave us what. That was fine with me. I didn't like even mentioning the dollar amounts of the gifts. As far I was concerned, everyone gave what they could, and it was the thought that counted.

Once Terry's family had gone through all the gifts and cards with us, and notated everything, they left. I was still exhausted from the festivities of the night before. But it was time to go pick up Jon Paul (nicknamed J.P.) from Lisa's sister Debbie's house. She had been kind enough to watch the baby for us on the wedding night.

I hated dropping off J.P. at the babysitter's when it was time to go to work. When I wasn't with him, I worried about him all the time. That way of life became too stressful, and Terry could see that. So, he agreed to let me put a hair salon in the basement of our house. That way, I could keep J.P. with me during the day and work from home.

That was fun for a while, and it kept me even busier than I needed to be. It was the perfect way for me to get acclimated to farm life. I got to keep the familiarity of doing hair while adjusting to the brand-new lifestyle that came with marrying Terry.

Living on the farm meant being more isolated than I had ever been. I was so used to running over to my mom's house two or three times a day. Now, I was stuck on farmland out in the middle of nowhere with Mom thirty-five minutes away.

I saw hair clients in my home five or six days a week. I also enrolled in the local community college to work on my bachelor's degree in art therapy. (I had taken classes prior to getting married.) Classes usually started at noon or 3:00. On the days I had classes, I cut hair in the evenings. I liked getting up every morning and having a purpose. I was used to being on a treadmill of activity and I liked being on the go.

One night about ten weeks into my marriage, the phone rang late at night. I had never liked getting late night calls. They were never good news. When the phone rang, I thought of the call I had gotten when Grandma died.

Mom called and told me, "Your dad, Richard, died."

"No, he didn't," I said, and hung up the phone. I couldn't accept that what she was saying was true.

Shortly before the wedding, Mom had read my tarot cards. I wanted reassurances about the baby, the wedding, and the marriage. One of the cards Mom turned over really stopped us in our tracks. It was the death card. It revealed that a tall, dark-haired man was going to die. I didn't know what to make of that prediction and I didn't really want to know. So, I blew it off and forgot about it.

Mom gave me five minutes to process the news and then called me back. She and J.R. were supposed to have visited Dad in South Dakota the weekend before. Something came up and they didn't end up going.

I thought back to my last few interactions with Dad. He had come over a couple of times when Jon Paul was still just a little baby. I had taken photos of Dad holding the baby. I also saw Dad at some point before the wedding. He was still living in South Dakota, but he had popped into town and stopped by my place to see me.

He was never big on communication, so we didn't talk much. That day was no different. We were just awkwardly standing around, making small talk. I was on my way out the door at the time. So, after a few minutes with Dad, I walked outside, loaded J.P. into his car seat, and told Dad I'd see him around.

As I pulled away from the house, Dad stood at the end of my driveway, watching me. It was so sad and weird. Usually, he could have cared less. He would have called me a dummy and taken off.

I saw him in my rearview mirror, just standing there, watching me. I kept waving at him, thinking, *Wow! Dad looks so sad! I wonder what's wrong.*

Dad terrorized us but we were his people, his family. We were all he really had in the world. You'd never know it by the way he treated us, but I know he loved us.

Then, right before the wedding, Dad called me from South Dakota. He was calling to talk, which was out of character for him. He was soft, nice and kind to me on the phone. This was totally unlike him. Usually, he would spend the conversation being sarcastic and making fun of people.

At the time of that call, I was mad at Dad. I'd heard through the grapevine that he'd been smack-talking me the last time he was in town. Dad was telling people that I didn't care about him because I didn't show up for his surgery in South Dakota.

He knew that I was in the hospital at the time, sick as a dog from the infection I got after giving birth. So, I couldn't understand why he was upset that I couldn't be in South Dakota for his surgery.

Dad had lost a finger in a work accident, and that's why he needed surgery. Or, that was his story, anyway. I had the feeling he'd cut off a body part just so he would be able to sue somebody. That was the kind of thing he would do. I was glad that he was living in South Dakota, far away from me. (He and my brother John had gone there for a construction job and Dad had stayed. That's where Dad claimed the work-related accident occurred.)

I rode up to the funeral home in South Dakota with my family. I really wanted Terry to go with me, but he said he would stay home and look after J.P. I said okay at the time, but it bothered me later. I wanted my husband with me on that trip.

On the way there, we were talking. "Maybe Dad was playing a trick on us, just to get us there so he could see us," I said. "Maybe he's planning to jump off the table when we get there and say, 'Just kidding!'"

We weren't a family that ever stayed mad at each other for very long. But this time, Dad couldn't get over his sadness and hurt. After being depressed for an entire week, he apparently overdosed on some combination of alcohol and pills. The pill bottle was found by his side.

I believe that Dad killed himself. He had never really gotten over the breakup with Mom. And I believe he missed us kids. I knew he was capable of killing himself because he had attempted it one day when he was in town, visiting from South Dakota. That time, he had also taken too many pills. On the night of that suicide attempt, he spent a lot of time on and off the phone with Mom.

They remained super close, and he monopolized her time. He was also friendly with J.R., but I think it was only so he could be close to Mom. Dad called Mom all the time and put a real strain on her marriage.

J.R. worked nights at a factory. For a while, he was assembling car doors, and then he got promoted to forklift driver. (Once he got injured, he could no longer be a jockey.) Dad would wait until he knew J.R. would be at work and then call Mom and talk to her for hours.

J.R. always felt that we kids intruded on the life he and Mom shared. He felt we were too dependent on Mom. But that was the nature of the relationship between us. That's why I loved how close Terry was to his family.

When we got to the funeral home, the mortician told us that we could see Dad before they cremated him. When he said that, suddenly reality hit me with so much force, I started to cry.

The guy from the morgue gave me the clothes Dad was wearing at the time of his death. His clothes smelled like cigarettes, beer and Brut After Shave.

When we saw Dad, he was lying on the table, cold, still and white. It was eerie to see his olive skin so pale. And it was strange to think this was the same man who had saved us so many times. I spent so much of my life either feeling threatened by Dad or being saved by him. He was always our savior.

Before I met Terry, Mom and J.R.'s house flooded due to a break in a dyke on the Platte River. The snows had begun to thaw and the whole area was flooded. The flood waters were so powerful, they knocked Mom's house right off the foundation.

By some miracle, Dad and Ricky happened to be visiting at the time. They were all sitting around, watching T.V. when water started pouring into the house. Dad went outside and found some people who had a small boat. By that time, Ricky had helped Mom and J.R. onto the roof. Dad got everybody to safety in the boat, taking them two at a time.

After we said our goodbyes at the funeral home, we went to Dad's apartment. He had a roommate who was a drinking buddy of his, and the guy happened to be from Columbus, Nebraska. The guy told us that Dad was mad at all of us. He said that Dad said we didn't love him.

The roommate started shaking a note in our face. Dad had left this handwritten note, written in crayon on the back of a keno ticket. It was his handwritten Last Will and Testament. In the note, he said he was leaving all his worldly possessions to his roommate. Believe it or not, that little note, written in crayon, on the back of a keno ticket, stood up in court.

I wanted to spend some time in Dad's room. So, I asked the man if I could get something of Dad's to remember him by. I said, "I want a shirt of my dad's!" I knew that any shirt of his would smell like him. I wanted to be able to bury my face in it and remember him by his scent.

While we were in Dad's room, I quietly told Ricky to look for a pawn ticket. Dad owned some diamonds. Well, they were actually Mom's diamonds. She had found them in a jewelry box in a garage sale. Dad scammed her out of the diamonds. Then he took them to a jewelry designer to get some jewelry made for himself. Dad was always dripping in gold and jewelry, like Mr. T.

I knew that when Dad was down and out and depressed, he went to the pawn shop. He was like that all my life. He would be doing really well for a while, and then doing really poorly.

"You look through the drawers," I said, "and I'll look in the closet. Let's see if we can find a pawn ticket."

Sure enough, Ricky found the pawn ticket in a drawer. Meanwhile, the roommate was ready to get us out of his apartment. So, he called the police on us. By the time the cops got there, we were on our way out the door.

THIRTY-THREE

NOT TOO LONG after the wedding, Terry, J.P. and I flew to Toledo, Ohio to see Daddy John. He looked very bloated and overweight. He was president of the union and that's all he wanted to talk about.

Daddy John enjoyed meeting Terry and J.P. He held the baby and played with him, and I could tell it meant a lot to him. When Terry and I were driving away, Daddy John cried like he loved me.

I said to myself, *He knows I'm his. He wouldn't be crying if he didn't care.*

Terry and I were staying at Grandma Lottie's house, so Terry got to meet Brenda. Over the years, Brenda and I had written letters back and forth. While we were at Grandma's, I also got a chance to interview her on videotape. Grandma talked about coming to America from Poland on a ship.

When we got back home, I showed Mom the photos of our trip. When she saw how bloated Daddy John looked, she said, "He's going to die soon. He's not healthy."

Mom talked about Daddy John having high blood pressure and being bloated. And she said she thought he might have been affected by all the chemicals he was around while working in the textile factory. My mother was right about Daddy John not being healthy. About six months after the trip, he died in his sleep of a brain aneurysm.

Mom told me that my brother John would be flying to the funeral, since he was Daddy John's son. I told her that I wanted to go too. I wanted to be there for Grandma Lottie and offer her my love and support. So, John and I flew to the funeral and stayed at Grandma Lottie's. It felt really good to be there for her.

I knew what a shock it was for her to lose her only son when he was only fifty-two years old. To outlive him was totally unnatural. Grandma was strong and brave in her grief—a real rock. It was a beautiful thing to witness.

I felt like my daddy issues were now behind me. I had outgrown the need for approval from my dads. I had a good man and I knew he was going to be a good father. Being with Terry on the farm, I felt like I was finally home.

Dad did raise me and provide for us. He was not the worst dad of all time, but he wasn't the daddy kind. I felt like Dad forever robbed me of having a father by taking his life. It made me really upset. I had always envisioned me and my brothers taking care of our parents in their old age.

I figured I'd be pushing Dad around in a wheelchair one day, on account of his back issues. Of course, Dad would have wanted no part of that. He ended his life just as he had lived it—on his own terms. He didn't care how much his actions hurt or bothered the family he left behind. That was typical of him.

Daddy John, on the other hand, had no control over his death. I was sad for his wife, Nancy, and their family.

I have come to realize that each person in my family makes me whole. I continue to draw from each of them. As I looked into Terry's green, glowing eyes, I felt like I was looking into a crystal ball. I could see and feel that I was home at last. The era of uncertainty, of so many moves from town to town and house to house, had come to an end. I am home in Terry's heart, in his family, and in the home he had built for us.

I feel like meeting me was the end of Terry's search for the other half of his heart, too. He wanted me and I was everything he needed. It was no longer *me* or *him*—it was going to be *us* forever. And we are home.

I thought back on all the times I tried to fit with someone who didn't fit me. I did it because they had it going on, or I thought they would be good for me. Being so fly-by-the-seat-of-my-pants by nature, I finally realized I needed to date guys who were stable and grounded. When I met Terry, I felt like I'd hit the jackpot. He was stable, grounded and entrepreneurial. I felt like he would understand me better than other guys, because I too had always been an entrepreneur.

Any time I get mad and think about leaving, I pull out our wedding tape and watch it. Terry is the rock that was worth waiting for—my big, strong, comforting man.

Then there's John, my older brother. In my family, I'm the mouth and my brother John is the muscle. He will always be the brave warrior. But, I'm mighty too, for a little person. Life made sure of that. I had to learn how to get in somebody's face and give them hell, if I wanted to survive. And I had to learn how to fight for my own safety against Dad.

My younger brother, Ricky, will always be the wise one. And my mother has always been my guardian angel. That was true while she was on earth and it is still true now that she's in Heaven.

I am not mad at my mom for moving all the time, or for not realizing that we kids desperately needed stability. I am not judging her for chasing a rainbow as she ran from Fred and into the path of fiery hell with Dad.

My mother died never knowing whether or not I was Daddy's John's daughter. And Daddy John died never knowing that I was not his daughter, after all. That's right—I was wrong about that!

I had always felt fairly sure that Daddy John was my dad. The only time I ever thought for one minute that maybe I wasn't Daddy John's was when I was nineteen. That's when Mom said I might be Fred's daughter. That didn't have much of an effect on me because of all the things Mom had said to me over the years that seemed to prove that I was definitely Daddy John's daughter.

She told me that Daddy John and I both had a rare blood type. We both had good leadership skills and were bossy. Daddy John was on the shorter side, so I thought that was another clue. (Then again, so was my mom.)

One day in early summer of 2018, I decided to find out for sure. So, I sent in DNA samples from me and my brother John. (I already knew that I wasn't my dad Richard's daughter so there was no reason to send in my brother Ricky's DNA sample.)

When the DNA results came back showing that my brother John and I did *not* share DNA, I was stunned. I couldn't wrap my brain around the fact that Daddy John was not my bio-father. That means that I am probably Fred's daughter.

In our lives, Fred was always the devil. He was the one we were running from all those years. Now that I know the truth, I am curious. I want to run to him and find out who he is, where he's from, and everything there is to know. I *need* to know more about him. Only then will I fully understand myself and make more sense to myself.

I do know that I am different, temperament-wise, from everyone else in my family. Take my temper, for example. I have the kind of temper where I can really hurt somebody. I can be dangerous when I get really angry.

I must have gotten that from Fred. I know I didn't get that from my mother. She was gentle and sweet all the time. I got that sweetness from my mom, but the rest of me is from Fred.

I started to wonder, *Did he do violent things all the time? Was he a lifetime criminal? Or was stabbing Mom a one-time thing? The attempted murder of Mom had to be premeditated, since he showed up at our door with a knife. But how did he get that mad?*

I also wonder, *Did Fred know I was his? Did he have any idea that I existed?*

I may never know. But if I did have these answers, then I would feel more complete, more at ease, and more peaceful.

Maybe Fred had other children. That would mean I have siblings, or nieces or nephews. I *love* family, and mine is so small. It would be great to discover more family members.

This is all new to me. In my heart, I am not afraid of Fred. My mind tells me that I probably should be. I can envision a scenario where he might try to hurt me simply because I reminded him of my mom.

Speaking of children, when J.P. was a teenager, he and Nels finally spoke by phone. Nels was doing well and had met someone special. His life was headed in a good direction.

Nels told me that he wanted the best for Jon Paul. He never tried to prevent Terry from being Jon Paul's father. Much later in J.P.'s life, he would connect with Nels and finally meet. Over time, they became close. But he would always consider Terry his dad.

AFTERWORD

EVERY LIFE IS different. It's like your own individual fingerprint. In every life, there is the good, the bad and the ugly. And we are each affected differently by the things that happen to us.

In my case, I don't trust easily. I always make sure to lock the doors at night. And I always have my car keys handy in case I need to make a quick getaway. I know that the boogie man could come in and get me while I'm sleeping. And, sometimes the biggest monster in your life is someone you love.

I still live in that turmoil every day. I don't trust people because they're going to get you. Every day, I worry about keeping my family and myself safe.

Whenever I'm in distress, I repeat my mom's words over and over. She always told me things like, "The sun is going to shine tomorrow. Tomorrow will be a better day. You'll see your life in a new light. Don't put a dark cloud on your future by dwelling on the past. Learn from it instead."

There are two sides to me. One side believes that the boogie man is going to come out at night. The other side of me wants to believe that the sun is going to come out tomorrow. Maybe that's why I always looked for the man in the moon. If I keep my focus on the man in the moon, the dark is not as black and empty.

When I grew up and started my married life as the wife of a farmer, I often felt isolated. Our land stretches for three counties and seems endless. As a farmer, my husband is often away from the house at night, working sometimes into the early morning. Nights can be scary and lonely.

Then one night, I opened the back door of the house and stepped outside. I saw the sky lit up like a million lightbulbs. There he was—so bright and close, I felt like I could touch him. The man in the moon! I had never seen the moon so clearly before.

I found comfort inside the shadows in the glowing ball in the sky. I said my prayers, thanking the Lord for all my blessings. And then I said goodnight to the man in the moon, knowing I would see my old friend again soon. As long as I know he will be waiting for me at night, I am never scared or lonely. I can always count on him.

ABOUT THE AUTHOR

SUZETTE SHANLE IS a college-educated farmer's wife and the mother of two daughters and one son. She is also a successful entrepreneur, a thirty-year hair stylist (retired), and beauty pageant winner.

She loves her family above all else, loves spending time with them, and looks forward to family vacations and other adventures. She is also a big animal lover and has been known to rescue a stray or two and make them part of the family.

The author believes in the words of her dearly departed mother: "We must learn to let go of past hurts and embrace tomorrow. For the sun will be out tomorrow, and it's sure to be a better day." Suzette also believes that we must learn to forgive ourselves. Only then can we forgive others.

She has not quite shaken her daddy issues, and one day hopes to meet her bio-father. Even if that day never comes, she fills her heart with the love she shares with her green-eyed husband, her beautiful daughters, and her veteran son. (And, of course, all the four-legged members of the family.)

Author's Note

THANK YOU FOR spending time with me and my family.
There was more to share than I could fit into one book. So, I'm adding volumes to this story. If you'll drop me a note at suzauthor@gmail.com, I'll keep you posted on future books. I would also love to hear how this book has touched your heart, and any stories you would like to share with me. I love connecting with my readers!

For now, stay strong and carry on. As my mother always told me, the sun will shine tomorrow, and it will be a better day.

Acknowledgments

I would like to acknowledge my developmental editor, Vivien Cooper, for guiding me through this book journey. Thank you for putting the puzzles pieces together to get my story written. Without your continuous guidance and support, I don't know if I would have finished this book.

I would also like to thank Elizabeth A. Dobbs for her talent and expertise in providing the artwork for the cover design.